THE TEMPTATION

THE TEMPTATIONS
OF
JESUS

by

VIC AUCOTT

The Christadelphian
404 Shaftmoor Lane
Hall Green
Birmingham B28 8SZ

2014

First published 2014

© 2014 The Christadelphian Magazine and Publishing Association

ISBN 978-0-85189-261-0

Printed and bound in Malta by
GUTENBERG PRESS LIMITED

CONTENTS

PREFACE

A S we contemplate the life of Jesus, and his triumph over temptation, we are overwhelmed by his single-mindedness and tenacity to achieve the victory. We are persuaded of his greatness as he combated the wrongs of his day to establish the righteousness of God. This mission could only lead to the cross. This was part of his burden, knowing how he would die as a young man, as a sacrifice for sin. In accomplishing this he lived in the spotlight of publicity. He was challenged by difficult situations and trick questions which tested his loyalty and citizenship, as well as by the enormity of the three wilderness temptations.

Invited to turn the stones into bread; being cajoled to jump off the highest corner pinnacle of the temple without injury to himself or his pride; to take the kingdoms of the world in exchange for the simple act of worshipping the tempter, are expressions of the Apostle John's explanation of sin. He tells us that "the lust of the flesh, and the lust of the eyes, and the pride of life" is "all that is in the world" (1 John 2:16).

The Temptations of Jesus explains how the three wilderness temptations fall into these three categories, as do the others which repeatedly tested Jesus during his ministry. The devil went away "for a season", but returned when Jesus subsequently faced testing. He appears to triumph so easily, but in reality it was all at great cost.

This book explores the journey of Jesus. It begins with an honest and hard look at the nature of temptation. It considers the purpose of the Jesus' baptism as he "fulfils all righteousness"; and describes the great and terrible wilderness with the difficulties of surviving forty days and nights. Each of the three specific temptations is dealt with in detail, and the narrative returns a number of times to 'the mind of the serpent' and its devious thinking, and how this might have had an influence on the mind of Jesus. The book considers the training of the Son of God which prepared him for his public ministry. What influences countered the thinking of the flesh? Where did this instruction come from? What was it? How was he encouraged to continue his life's work, given the impediments and hardships he endured? Jesus is the Son of God, a unique Son. The relationship he enjoyed with his Father was close, intimate and loving, and this answers some of our questions, but not all.

This study began as a nine-part series of Bible Class talks over three years. As the talks proceeded, the experience helped me to get closer to the person of the Lord Jesus, and to know even better his greatness, generosity and most of all his love. The original talks have been extended to provide a more 'rounded' approach to this vitally important subject, and the whole is now offered to encourage others to share the same experiences of wonder and joy. May we be helped to know ourselves as we are known, and truly appreciate what has been accomplished for us.

VIC AUCOTT
Nottingham
April 2014

1

THE NATURE OF TEMPTATION

THE spiritually-minded and holy Son of God was sensitive to the onslaught of evil against himself, but especially against his Father. The separateness and holiness of the name of the God of Israel was to be defended against defilement by blasphemy and slander, or by disobedience and wrongdoing, by speaking the truth.

Likewise the beloved Son, who grew up under the shadow of the wings of his Father and waxed strong in spirit, filled with wisdom, and upon whom was the grace of God, would not be deflected from the course his Father had set him. The honour, glory, power and might that belonged to the Father were not to be snatched away by either the lust of the flesh, the lust of the eyes or the pride of life (1 John 2:16) or by any person, or however these things were manifested.

These studies

These temptation studies attempt in a very cautious way to get close to the mind of Jesus, and to understand his thought processes. We shall recreate as far as possible the Biblical scenes which reveal the Lord's attitude and deportment when involved in difficult and tempting situations, learn from his responses and wonder at his strength of mind. We shall tread very carefully and as reverently as possible, as we explore the conception of the 'temptations', and consider his God-fearing and scriptural answers. How was it possible for Jesus to have such thoughts, if that was the case, as might lead him to breach his commitment to his Father as both Son and Servant?

Human nature and its problems

The question is often asked, 'Was it possible for Jesus to have sinned?', and the answer is a resounding 'Yes!', because he had the same nature as ourselves. The next question is, 'But how was it possible for Jesus to sin?' and the answer is, because there was in him and an integral part of him, a law, a principle, a force, or the power of 'sin'. "He hath made him to be sin for us", the scriptures tell us. This is not a reference to any personal individual mistakes and sins, for Jesus did not commit any sin, but to the nature which Jesus had and we all have, and to the law which drives the 'sinning' process forwards, and converts lust into mistakes and sins. There is quite a difference between the two.

We know it better as the impulses or the urges to do wrong. By these we are drawn away. We have these impulses built into us from birth and that determines what we are, weak corruptible human beings. We cannot help that. It has been called "our misfortune". What we do with those impulses is crucial. If we allow them free rein, we commit sin. In Jesus' case he not only controlled all the impulses, he defeated them, rejected them, denied the lust its conception and so did no personal sin. That's the difference between him and us.

"In all points"

In Hebrews 4:15 we read that in Jesus the Son of God, "we have not an high priest which cannot be touched with the feeling of our infirmities; but was in all points tempted like as we are, yet without sin".

What does it mean, "in all points"? Does it mean he was tempted in every possible situation in which believing saints have sinned or are likely to sin, in order to understand our feelings and needs? Or does it mean he was tempted in a similar fashion, by the same process, but not necessarily encompassing each and every one of our temptations? The Emphatic Diaglott literal translation for Hebrews 4:15 is: "... having been tempted but all things according to a likeness, apart from sin". The English translation is put as, "... but one

2

having been tried in all respects like ourselves, apart from sin". The crucial words are "in all respects".

There is a useful piece written by Brother Robert Roberts in *The Christadelphian*. It is part of an answer to a correspondent in which, inter alia, he discussed the nature of Christ. He wrote:

"Both John and Paul place the nature of Christ in the position of a first principle, on which there is to be no compromise. John says that no man is to be received who denies that Jesus came *in the flesh* (1 John 4:3; 2 John 10); and Paul is careful to emphasise that the flesh in question was 'of the seed of David' (2 Timothy 2:8; Romans 1:3); derived from which, he necessarily partook of 'the same' flesh and blood as his brethren (Hebrews 2:14), and was consequently 'tempted in all points like them', though without sin (4:15) ... The very essence of temptation is susceptibility to wrong suggestion. The victory lies in the opposing considerations brought to bear.

"The truth of the matter does not depend upon the word 'likeness' or any other single term, but upon the combination of statements made – which are all in language plain enough to be free from obscurity. At the same time, it has to be pointed out that the word 'likeness' in the Greek has the force of resemblance so complete as to be sameness. This is illustrated in the statement that Jesus was made in 'the likeness of men' (Philippians 2:7). The extent of the likeness is defined as extending to 'all points' and 'all things' (Paul's words – Hebrews 2:17, 4:15). What can we say but that he was a man, and not the mere likeness of a man?"[1]

We remember the words in Hebrews 2:17,18: "Wherefore in all things it behoved him to be made like unto his brethren ... For in that he himself hath suffered being tempted, he is able to succour them that are tempted". This doesn't mean that the Lord Jesus suffered every same individual evil impulse which

1 *The Christadelphian*, Volume 32, 1895, page 63.

deflects us from the way of righteousness. Rather, that he had propensities which were susceptible to the influences of temptation common to man, and which fall under three separate categories: "the lust of the flesh, and the lust of the eyes, and the pride of life".

The answer

The mind is like a sponge and all kinds of messages and images are soaked up, sometimes unintentionally, sometimes unknowingly, sometimes deliberately. Then they come to the fore. How we deal with these things is crucial. We know only too well the deviousness of our thought processes, and the ease with which we can get carried from one thought to another, without really thinking about it. To have an evil thought is not to sin, providing the thought is rejected quickly. Occasionally we are successful in doing this. We may find it hard to understand that Jesus could have had similar thoughts. This does not diminish the stature of the Lord Jesus Christ, but rather enhances it.

The wonder is that he was able to repulse all the wrong thoughts which ever entered his heart, and was still without sin, because lust, that inordinate desire which was in him, as it is in the rest of us, was not allowed to conceive. It was a battle of wills, a battle for the mind, a battle of spirit and flesh. Jesus was triumphant.

The nature of Christ

In dealing with the nature of Jesus and its relationship to his temptations, together with his daily trials and ordinary troubles and concerns of the flesh, we must take into account the wide sweep of scripture and the way the apostles expressed their teaching. As Brother Robert Roberts wrote, it is a first principle.

Initially we must consider what Jesus said about his own nature. We get part of the answer when he responded to the question put by the certain ruler who came running and kneeled before him and asked, "Good Master, what good thing shall I do that I may have eternal life?" Before answering this question, Jesus dealt with the appellation, "Good Master". All three synoptic writers record his reply in the same form: "Why callest thou me good? there is none good but one, that is, God" (Matthew 19:17; Mark 10:18; Luke 18:19). Jesus was not referring to his way of life, or the pattern of his behaviour, or his morality, or how he lived day by day. It was not about the quality of his life, for he could say without embarrassment, "Which of you convinceth me of sin?" (John 8:46). In responding to the certain ruler Jesus was talking about his nature, and as God is the only 'good One', then his own nature was inherently flawed and not yet perfected, and therefore capable of fault, error or sin. So Jesus confesses his humanity and weakness.

But he rightly emphasises the true, righteous and holy nature of his Father, the eternal Spirit, and "who alone has immortality, dwelling in light which no man can approach unto ... nor can see" (1 Timothy 6:16). At the time Jesus spoke the words, only God was good in the ultimate sense by having the inherent moral authority to make righteous judgements. "Shall not the Judge of all the earth do right?" confessed Abraham (Genesis 18:25).

The apostolic evidence is just as decisive. The apostles underline the inherent capacity of Jesus to human weakness, by writing of the days of his flesh. A selection of appropriate scriptures will demonstrate this:

"... that of the fruit of [David's] loins, according to the flesh, [God] would raise up Christ ..." (Acts 2:30)

"God sending his own Son in the likeness of sinful flesh, and for sin, condemned sin in the flesh ..."
(Romans 8:3)

"God sent forth his Son, made of a woman, made under the law ..." (Galatians 4:4)

"For he made him to be sin for us, who knew no sin." (2 Corinthians 5:21)

"... make the captain of their salvation perfect through sufferings." (Hebrews 2:10)

5

"Every spirit that confesseth that Jesus Christ is come in the flesh is of God." (1 John 4:2)

Another helpful article by Brother Harry Tennant appeared under the title, "The Nature of Christ" in *The Testimony* magazine. He wrote about the things Jesus experienced in his life, why they were there and how he dealt with them. Although the three wilderness temptations were not specifically mentioned, the points made were pertinent. A flavour of the article follows:

"The battle was to be fought on the territory of sin and death, and not remotely in some other way. Furthermore, it was no mechanical achievement brought about by effortless work. It was to be accomplished by Christ's being touched with our infirmities and tempted in all points like his brethren (Hebrews 4:15)."

"There can be no doubt that the Lord was a man of fellow feeling. He was in 'all things ... made like unto his brethren (Hebrews 2:17)."

"From time to time some brethren, whilst giving ready assent to this teaching, have held back from its deeper implications. All of the experiences ... were possible because Christ was mortal.

"It appears to have been from a mistaken regard for the person of Christ that some brethren have shrunk from applying these words to Jesus; or, if they have applied them, they have sought to redefine 'sinful flesh' by saying that we do not inherit a bias toward sin. We believe that this is to misunderstand both the nature of Christ and the nature of his atoning work."

"In ways beyond our experience [Jesus] knew altogether what was in man, and that included knowledge of himself as a man. His mind was the battle ground between the law that was in his members and those things which were of his Father. These were not two separate persons within him, two

6

separate parts; they were the ingredients of his one nature."[2]

The nature of man

As we work through these studies we shall visit some familiar scripture passages, and be reminded of the fundamental teaching about our own nature and the process of temptation. We shall begin at the heart of the matter because this is where all sin begins, and we must make it personal if we are going to benefit.

"The heart is deceitful above all things, and desperately wicked: who can know it?"

(Jeremiah 17:9)

The answer to the question raised by the prophet is 'the only one who really knows it, is the Lord Jesus Christ'. The rest of us fail to understand fully and deal adequately with our heart's desires and so are deceived by them. The heart is the mind. It's the place where thoughts begin and are processed, which then mature and are expressed. The heart expresses what we are, the essence of ourselves. It controls the psyche and lets us know about ourselves. But it's flawed. It's deceitful: in fact, "deceitful above all things and desperately sick". It is terminally ill, struggling and fighting for survival. And how it fights!

"Deceitful" means beguiling, deceiving, crooked, polluted. It comes from a root word meaning 'to seize by the heel', and the first thing we note is how the heart is linked to the serpent and its attitude. It tries to be one thing but it is really another. It pretends integrity, faithfulness and truth, but in reality it is anything but, naturally speaking. It causes us to do wrong, think that which is wrong, to be wrong. There is worse to come. There is nothing more beguiling in the whole world than our own heart, because "it is deceitful above all things". It is by far the greatest deceiver we shall ever have to confront.

The Gospel of Christ sets the perfect standard of behaviour, but it also teaches us that we cannot

2 *The Testimony*, July 1988, pages 234-237.

reach that high moral standard whilst in the flesh. Therefore falling short of the Gospel of Christ means sin is committed; sometimes unintentionally, sometimes deliberately, but most times unthinkingly. At those times we make our choices and lust is in full flood – we are entangled in the froth of excitement as well as enticement.

But we don't like to think like this. We prefer not to think it's so brutal and stark, that we could be so easily swept along in a tide of self-gratification, when we know or ought to know better. But that is the deceitfulness of the human heart or mind. It can convince us that we are doing no wrong, even when we are enjoying the pleasures of sin for a season. It will beguile us into believing that wrong is right, or that sin is simply harmless fun and relaxation, with no harm done.

We can believe this and sink back contentedly in our own self-deception and false security, until we wake up spiritually, and see the wonder of the righteousness and the holiness of Christ, and the horror of what we really are and perhaps have done. But initially we are driven by self-indulgence and self-survival, naturally speaking. Even though we are brethren and sisters in Christ, and know a better way, the fact remains that the "old man" is still very much alive; even though we once publicly crucified him with all his affections and lusts at our baptisms, and try to do so on a daily basis as best we can. 'The heart is deceitful, the heart is seizing us by the heel and desperately evil'. It is very serpentine in behaviour. And who can know it? We know our hearts no better than Eve knew the serpent.

The Apostle James tells us:

"Let no man say when he is tempted, I am tempted of God: for God cannot be tempted with evil, neither tempteth he any man: but every man is tempted, when he is drawn away of his own lust, and enticed. Then when lust hath conceived, it bringeth forth sin: and sin, when it is finished, bringeth forth death."

(James 1:13-15)

"Every man"! This is totally inclusive and without any exception or distinction. James explains the 'mechanics' of temptation. It is the result of desire drawing us away and enticing us. Yet desire can also be natural and honourable. It springs from within, in order to satisfy real needs to ensure the continuation of life. For example, working, feeding and loving. Yet the key here is the expression "drawn away". The words suggest a movement, a change in our focus, thinking differently, wanting something else. It's a shift in priorities, however momentary. The apostle was thinking of the Christian believer who can be "drawn away" from his secure position in the faith of the Lord Jesus Christ, by unholy desire and lust which springs into the mind, sometimes unbidden, but nevertheless dangerous. The desire grows so large like an unwelcome cancer, that it can obscure our God-centred thoughts, and obliterates their good effect on the conscience.

We are led by this process into carnal things, having been "drawn away" from spiritual things. It doesn't matter what the issue is, the process is always the same. We know this. It is our daily experience and conflict. It may be somewhat artificial to mark a point in these three verses in James, to try and decide where in the process described we reach the point of no return, and inevitably fall into sin. Is it when we are "drawn away"? Or is it during the enticement, when the natural man is stimulated? Or is it in the conceiving? It could well vary, with people having different strengths, weaknesses and susceptibilities. Some may be able to apply the brake of self-control early, some at other stages, while others cannot resist the tension of the moment and yield to the pressure, because of their Achilles heel. Sin is committed.

2

EVIL THINGS COME FROM WITHIN

D URING one of Jesus' many confrontations with the Pharisees, chief priests, lawyers and scribes, questions arose around the person and authority of John the Baptist. It was about his preaching and the response which was anticipated from those who heard it and knew it to be true. The common people and the sinners believed John's message and "justified God" by being baptized:

> "But the Pharisees and lawyers rejected the counsel of God against themselves, being not baptized of him." (Luke 7:30)

Self-justification

It was this rejection which prompted Jesus to comment on their position. It came down to them being described as spoiled children who would not join in other children's games although they were invited, and slandering John the Baptist for his eating habits and the company he kept. When Luke records Jesus' words that "wisdom is justified of all her children" (7:35), there is an added dimension when we recall that 'justify' means 'to declare right'. This can mean that not only God Himself, but also John and Jesus are all declared to be 'right', both in the message they presented and the salvation they offered. The wisdom from above would and could justify the children of wisdom. This witness is true.

However there is an equally valid but complementary understanding of these same words, when applied to the Pharisees and lawyers in their opposition to the Gospel of God and the baptism of John. Jesus was constrained to conclude, because of their manifest intransigence and rebellious attitude, and their refusal to recognise

10

and accept him as the long promised Messiah, that their "wisdom is justified of all her children". The evidence was in front of them, but as religious masters they knew better! They would have no difficulty in justifying to themselves that their refusal of John the Baptist, and therefore of Jesus of Nazareth, was right! They would "take counsel together against the LORD and against his anointed" on many occasions during Jesus' ministry, and so the art of self-justification became finely tuned. This is a human failing, and it breeds false reasoning and pride. The Apostle Paul put it succinctly in Romans 12:16, "Be not wise in your own conceits".

The tragedy is that at times human wisdom is justified of all her children. We can justify anything we want to do, think or say. We can convince ourselves we are not doing wrong, because our deceitful heart is telling us it is right! What is sinful becomes right, because the conscience is seared, and we become immune to iron burn and injury! We are experts at self-deception. We have been doing it from our earliest days of childhood! We can easily justify what we want to do, until by a disciplined process of learning and training we develop a spiritual mind, which enables us to discern between right and wrong when we remember to apply the nobler principles to the situation. If we are truly honest with ourselves, even if sometimes we are not with each other, we allow the natural man to become dominant some of the time. That's because we make wrong choices, and like it that way. Sin gives us pleasure and is attractive. So, "wisdom is justified of all her children", for 'the heart is seizing us by the heel and is desperately wicked'.

Worldly thinking

All of this is the way of the world. It manifests itself in our personal behaviour.

This was a serious problem in the Corinthian ecclesia and was vigorously addressed by the Apostle Paul:

"Know ye not that ye are the temple of God, and that the Spirit of God dwelleth in you? If any man defile the temple of God, him shall God destroy; for

11

the temple of God is holy, which temple ye are. Let no man deceive himself." (1 Corinthians 3:16-18)

Paul refers to defiling the temple of God. We could see this only as a reference to the sexual perversions and immorality of Corinth, and how this behaviour defiled the holy bodies of the saints in that city. Paul was going to apply a censure later in his letter over this matter. But this understanding is not necessarily the only one we should apply to the passage. He is certainly speaking of personal and individual bodies. In these bodies live the enduring principles and precepts of God, when we have rightly understood and absorbed them, following our repentance and baptism. But our bodies are earthen vessels, capable of cracking, leaking or breaking, as well as absorbing external influences. Defilement is therefore anything which mars the glory of God residing in these earthen vessels:

"Let no man deceive himself. If any man among you seemeth to be wise in this world, let him become a fool, that he may be wise. For the wisdom of this world is foolishness with God. For it is written, He taketh the wise in their own craftiness. And again, The Lord knoweth the thoughts of the wise, that they are vain. Therefore let no man glory in men." (verses 18-21)

There are echoes here from Genesis 3 – "deceive", "wise", "world", "craftiness", "vain". So the self-justification we project when "wisdom is justified of all her children", is serpent-like in character. We project a denial of the word of God, and run counter to it. We know the faults of the serpent, and rightly condemn them and the serpent for its evil – but beware, we do the same. To protest otherwise is to be beguiled by a heart which is "deceitful above all things and desperately wicked": the heart has seized us by the heel.

The Apostle John has something to say about self-deception:

"If we say that we have no sin, we deceive ourselves, and the truth is not in us." (1 John 1:8)

12

"If we say that we have not sinned, we make him a liar, and his word is not in us." (verse 10)

This is an important lesson. Sin doesn't stop because we are baptized and in Christ. The lasting and condemning effects of sin are changed, for we have passed from death to life, but our nature remains the same. To a greater or lesser degree our thinking is the same. We wish it was altogether different but we do have advantages now that we didn't have before baptism, as John also wrote:

"If we confess our sins, he is faithful and just to forgive us our sins, and to cleanse us from all unrighteousness." (verse 9)

That is crucial for our eternal welfare, but we need to "confess our sins". How we confess, and what we actually confess is not for exploring now. What we are concerned with now is the possibility – and because the Spirit through the Apostle John saw fit to raise this matter specifically, the probability – of denying the problem of sin, and therefore temptation in our lives: as if somehow, all is now well with the world and ourselves, because the Lord Jesus Christ came into the world to save sinners, died and rose again, and we are 'in him', and therefore safe.

Only to a limited extent is this true. We should be confident and firm believers in the certainty of eternal salvation for those who by faithful lives, "abide in him". Further, there should be no fear at the judgement seat, "for if our heart condemn us, God is greater than our heart, and knoweth all things" (1 John 3:20) and, "Herein is our love made perfect, that we may have boldness in the day of judgment: because as he is, so are we in this world" (4:17). In the passage from 1 John 1 quoted above, the apostle used the language of Genesis 3 and the serpent when he wrote about "no sin ... deceive ... truth is not in us ... liar ... his word is not in us". These are some of the elements which caused the downfall of Adam and Eve, and John was careful to ensure that his believing children did not follow their carnal example. A denial of personal sin negates the continuing ministry of the Lord Jesus Christ as a faithful and merciful High Priest. The key words in all this are "deceive ourselves". That happens when our heart has seized us by the heel.

The world we live in

"Love not the world, neither the things that are in the world. If any man love the world, the love of the Father is not in him. For all that is in the world, the lust of the flesh, and the lust of the eyes, and the pride of life, is not of the Father, but is of the world."
(1 John 2:15,16)

John says, "Love not the world", and tells us the reason why. The world we are not to love is the source of lust and pride. But in his Gospel he writes that "God so loved the world". Which world is John thinking about in his letter and how can we decide whether we should 'love' or 'love not'?

The Greek word for "world" in each of the five occurrences in these two verses is *kosmos*. It has various shades of meaning and is understood as, 'to set in order', 'the orderly arrangements [of society]', 'the world as it is shaped'. It includes the inhabitants and the organisation, with its order, but the general application is to the whole creation in its natural condition and separated by sin from God. *Kosmos* comes from a root from which derives the English word 'cosmetic', and explains why 'decoration' and 'adorning' are among the meanings offered in the concordances. John employs *kosmos* twenty-three times in this first epistle and nearly eighty times in the Gospel. His use of the word is more than all the other New Testament writers combined. The apostle is considering the disordered world in its relationship with God and the divine prerogative of righteousness and judgement. To John, the *kosmos* meant the prevailing unspiritual and immoral order of human affairs, particularly the Jewish world and its society, the arrangements of which were hostile to God and if they remain unchanged would be outside the orbit of His salvation.

14

Yet it is the same world that "God so loved" and that He gave His only begotten Son to die for. It is the world of mortal, dying men and women which God loves and Jesus died to save, and in this sense only, we as His children must also love, so as to pull some out of the fire. This same world is driven by principles and forces which God by His very nature rejects, and we must also resist, or we cannot be His children. James refers to these principles and forces when he instructs us that "friendship of the world is enmity with God" (4:4), and John has them in mind when he writes, "Love not the world, neither the things that are in the world", and then tells us that the "things" are "the lust of the flesh, and the lust of the eyes, and the pride of life".

John is denouncing the world in its natural sinful state, separated from God because it is "lying in the power of the evil one" (1 John 5:19, John 14:30). It is a world which is filled with lust and vanity, and having desires which are contrary to those who are born of God and have become the children of God. It is society orientated against God and by its very nature hostile to the Being and love of God. This is the unspiritual world we must not love, but reject. We must resist the inbred and unregenerate impulses and passions which make the world what it is – godless, pagan and corrupt. It is manifested by "the lust of flesh, and the lust of the eyes, and the pride of life".[1]

But it is not human existence per se that is condemned by John; the world of physical activity and daily work, and the means by which most of us earn a living; or even the social interaction in the home and with neighbours, or with the wider family if they do not share our precious faith. As children of God we must love the sinner, but hate all evil and sin and be separate from it.

The trouble is that lust is bred by the world in which we live. It is always there, part of the fabric of society.

---

1   These ideas are more fully developed in Brother Neville Smart's book, *The Epistles of John*, pages 56,57, and in *Fellowship in the Life Eternal – an exposition of the Epistles of St. John*, 1909 edition, pages 196,197, by George G. Findlay DD.

It is as if lust is in the very air we breathe: it feeds our appetites, our desires and our egos; that is our flesh, our eyes, our pride. These are the three most powerful natural drivers for survival. The world and its inherent lust will pass away, says John, but meanwhile the instinct for survival is fed by these natural lusts. We cannot escape them.

One of our brethren has written very poignantly about the believers' relationship with the world:

"One unanswerable argument against worldliness is that if we love the world, the love of the Father is not in us; the two are mutually exclusive. Jesus virtually says the same thing when he says, 'Ye cannot serve God and mammon'. It is important to notice that he does not say we *must* not, but we *cannot*: it is an impossibility ... And John ... asserts that 'God is light, and in him is no darkness at all'; and to claim fellowship with him whilst walking in the darkness of the world is to expose ourselves as liars ...

"[The] imperative to 'Love not the world' is pertinent to us all, not only because of the subtle dangers to which the children of God are exposed, but also because, although Christ has overcome the world, the full effects of his victory will only be seen when God's purpose is complete ... Any compromise the believer makes with the world diminishes the power of Christ in the eyes of men. The world is not a theological concept to use as a contrast to the ways of God, so much as the very real pagan background against which the Christian must live his life of godly service and witness ... When our witness falls on deaf ears and the blows we strike for our Lord seem to be a mere beating of the air, it is all too easy for us to relax and only conform as much as is comfortably possibly to our Christian standards ... It is altogether right that John's exhortation should be expressed in the stern imperative, 'Love not the world'."[2]

2 Brother Melva Purkis, *First Epistle of John,* 1988, published by CIL, pages 49-51.

(i) Lust of flesh:

This has little to do with how our material bodies are kept alive by food and drink. John is thinking about the ways and thoughts in which the flesh expresses itself and satisfies the appetites. It's about how we seek self-gratification at every turn and how we want to do our own thing and get our own way. It's about how we have what we want.

(ii) Lust of the eyes:

Through the eyes we see and desire; we covet and want. In our stronger moments we remember that covetousness is idolatry. We feed our flesh appetites with wants in excess of our needs. We build our barns in which to store our increased goods, forgetting the wisdom of the New Testament that "godliness with contentment is great gain" (1 Timothy 6:6), and "be content with such things as ye have" (Hebrews 13:5). We sometimes substitute the "exceeding and eternal weight of glory" for the transient and the glittering, because we can have it now; and the eternal, in these weaker moments, seems so far away. At times we prefer what we can see and hold, rather than the things that are not seen. So we have it now, having been enticed by the lust of the eyes.

(iii) Pride of life:

This is our ego: it's our sense of self-importance. This is vaunting and parading of self, the puffing up of self. It is glorying in our own power and achievements, either subconsciously or otherwise, seeking to be as gods. This is the most basic and powerful of all the 'things of the world' which we should resist. All our other lusts come from this inflated and conceited view of ourselves, which has an insatiable appetite for personal satisfaction and self-fulfilment. In satisfying our passions and lusts there is sin, when we take and have unlawfully or unwisely. This was the evil which caused Adam and Eve to "be as gods, knowing good and evil", and to seek equality with God.

Adam, Eve and the serpent

The order in which John presents his summary of our
nature and inherent weaknesses, "the lust of the flesh,
and the lust of the eyes, and the pride of life" which is
"of the world", is consistent with those stages involved
in Eve's temptation by the serpent, and matched by the
narrative of Genesis 3:

> "And the serpent said unto the woman, Ye shall not
> surely die: for God doth know that in the day ye eat
> thereof, then your eyes shall be opened, and ye shall
> be as gods, knowing good and evil. And when the
> woman saw that the tree was good for food, and that
> it was pleasant to the eyes, and a tree to be desired to
> make one wise, she took of the fruit thereof, and did
> eat, and gave also unto her husband with her; and he
> did eat. And the eyes of them both were opened, and
> they knew that they were naked."   (verses 4-7)

We are familiar with the first part of the conversation
(verses 2,3) between Eve and the serpent, and how
Eve's response was not the whole truth of what the
angel had instructed, and how the serpent led her into
a false position by lying to her. It made a promise it
couldn't keep, and offered prospects of glory, privilege
and responsibility it couldn't deliver. The serpent
did so without warning her of the consequences and
successfully beguiled Eve to cheat on God, then covet
and grasp at equality which was not hers to have, and
not the serpent's to promise or to give. She was totally
unprepared for the subtlety of the temptation. Equality
with God is in the gift of God; it was not to be snatched
at or taken.

The way verse 6 is worded in the Authorised Version
instructs us about the component parts of temptation,
as the following table illustrates:

Genesis 3:6	1 John 2:16
saw the tree was *good for food*	the lust of the flesh

it was pleasant [a *desire* – AV margin] to *the eyes*	the lust of the eyes
a tree to be desired *to make one wise* [:5, as gods]	the pride of life

Eve was deceived by assertions and prospects that were false. Consequently, to satisfy this desire to be made wise, and to be as the angels knowing good and evil, she "took of the fruit thereof, and did eat, and gave also unto her husband with her; and he did eat". They saw, desired and took. They were disobedient to God. Death followed as a consequence of their sin. Part of what the serpent promised came true because their eyes *were* opened, but that brought unexpected problems. They knew they were naked and became ashamed and hid themselves. Their awareness of each other had been aroused, and they provided their own fig leaf covering. Adam and Eve were separated from God and attempted to remedy their physical nakedness themselves, whereas God by sacrifice was prepared to cover their moral poverty, and rebuild the broken relationship caused by this sin.

Saw, desired and took

This sequence of "saw", "desired", "took" is repeated a number of times in the Old Testament. The instances are concerned with wrong choices, which brought disaster for those involved. There follows now a series of five such cases, to illustrate the seriousness of wrong choices and the consequences for each one who was involved.

"The sons of God saw the daughters of men that they were very fair [pleasing, pleasant, desirable]; and they took them wives of all which they chose."

(Genesis 6:2)

Death followed some 120 years or so later as Genesis 6:13 and 7:22 make clear, because these brethren followed the pattern of temptation established in the

Garden of Eden and turned the antediluvian ecclesial world on its head. They saw, desired, and took.

"And Lot lifted up his eyes, and beheld all the plain of Jordan, that it was well watered everywhere, before the LORD destroyed Sodom and Gomorrah, even as the garden of the LORD, like the land of Egypt, as thou cometh unto Zoar. Then Lot chose him all the plain of Jordan; and Lot journeyed east: and they separated themselves the one from the other."

(Genesis 13:10,11)

Lot was seeking the comfort of the well watered plains near to Sodom, for this temptation is about the desire for comfort and the good life. He lifted up his eyes, beheld and chose. He followed the same sequence as the first pair, and death and destruction in Sodom and Gomorrah came some thirty to forty years later as Genesis 13:13 and 19:24,25 explain.

"And when Shechem the son of Hamor the Hivite, prince of the country, saw her [Dinah], he took her, and lay with her, and defiled her. And his soul clave unto Dinah the daughter of Jacob, and he loved the damsel, and spake kindly unto the damsel."

(Genesis 34:2,3)

Shechem's forcing of Dinah is about the lust of the flesh, for he saw her, took her, and loved her. Here was uncontrolled passion driven by a desire that in different circumstances would have been honourable. But the haste and fulfilment of the lust resulted in enticement leading Shechem into wrongdoing. Death followed when the two brothers of Dinah took immediate revenge with the sword.

[Achan said] "When I saw among the spoils a goodly Babylonish garment, and two hundred shekels of silver, and a wedge of gold of fifty shekels weight, then I coveted them, and took them; and, behold, they are hid in the earth in the midst of my tent, and the silver under it." (Joshua 7:21)

Achan's stealing of the silver, the golden wedge and a garment from Jericho is about the desire for personal wealth, greed and having something at the expense of someone else. God had been denied His consecrated and devoted offerings, for Israel had been specifically charged with placing the spoils of war from both Jericho and Ai into the tabernacle treasury. Achan reproduced the pattern of sin of Adam and Eve. "I saw ... I coveted ... and took". His death followed immediately by stoning and burning in a summary judgement.

These four references have confirmed the pattern of temptation – that it is no different whatever the sin. All sin follows this sequence of seeing, desiring and taking. Whether the issue is wealth, possessions, other women, or the desire to be different, it means having something which is unwise, and which may belong to someone else, and there are breaches of the law of God. In all cases death followed sooner or later.

But we are all guilty of this in one degree or another, and none is excluded. We all see, desire, take, and it does not matter even if we think the situation is only minor. It can be sinful thought leading to sinful behaviour. It may mean someone somewhere is robbed. In these four cases, God is robbed of His honour because the sons of God looked outside the ecclesia for wives; Abraham is robbed of a companion in the journey of faith and hope; Dinah of her virginity and integrity; God of His devoted offerings. All wilfulness will hurt God when He is set aside by self-indulgence. When we sideline Him, we presumptuously put ourselves centre stage. We attempt to act as gods professing to know good and evil and what is good for ourselves and others.

We could add to these powerful examples illustrations from the book of Judges concerned with the experiences of Samson, which follow this same pattern. For the sake of brevity the scripture references only are given, but "saw", "desire", "took" is plainly seen.

Judges 14:1 – "saw"; verse 3 – "pleaseth me well", desire; verse 8 – "to take her".

Judges 16:1 – "saw"; "went in unto her", desire; and took in one unwise act.

In these two cases Samson was drawn away by women, although he was able to escape the natural consequence of death. In yet another encounter he paid the ultimate price for entwining himself with Delilah, who herself demonstrated this subtle process in her seduction and entrapment of Samson:

Judges 16:5 – "give thee silver", saw; verse 5 – "entice him", desire; verse 18 – "showed me all his heart", took him.

The fifth illustration is equally powerful, as it demonstrates the ease and wilfulness with which the sin process is set in motion. It concerns King David:

"And it came to pass in an eveningtide, that David arose from off his bed, and walked upon the roof of the king's house: and from the roof he saw a woman washing herself; and the woman was very beautiful to look upon. And David sent and inquired after the woman. And one said, Is not this Bathsheba, the daughter of Eliam, the wife of Uriah the Hittite? And David sent messengers, and took her; and she came in unto him, and he lay with her; for she was purified from her uncleanness: and she returned unto her house."   (2 Samuel 11:2-4)

Here is the sequence again – "saw", "look" (desire), "took her". What David did was no different in the behaviour pattern to those mentioned in the four earlier examples. In David's case the event became public knowledge with dreadful consequences. If we behave as these others we can try to keep it hidden pretending there are no consequences. At best this is hypocritical, when we are all guilty of the same sin process. As before, death followed the sin (see 2 Samuel 11:17; 12:19). But this time it was the lawful husband and the love child. Because it was so serious David was severely censured, whereas we might think we have got away with it because there is no immediate judgement. But this is "the heart [which] is deceitful above all things" beguiling us into thinking that wrong is right, and seizing us by the heel.

When we condemn a man like David for his behaviour, we are also condemning ourselves, because we go down a similar road, following the same pattern of seeing, desiring, and taking. We do this daily, although the offence might not be as serious. Yet God forgave David following his repentance and confession. God through Christ has been pleased to forgive us our faults when we profess our faith and make our confessions; so we ought to be equally gracious in accepting the confessions and repentances of our fallen brethren and sisters when they present themselves. It doesn't matter what the issue is. Our personal preferences should not get in the way.

Conclusion

This pattern of temptation is set in our own hearts. We are no different from any others, except that in some, there may be degrees of self-control which cover up or prevent the worst excesses. But sin is sin, and none of us has any room or right to think worse of another. For there are no shades of sin in the eyes of God. This is the horror story of human nature, what we are really like, and how easy it is to follow the same pattern of temptation – "see", "desire", "take". We keep it in check as best we can, through our belief and appreciation of the Gospel and the person and work of the Lord Jesus Christ. It is because of this that we need not beat ourselves unnecessarily. We know there is a beautiful remedy to our horror story. We are not held responsible for our natures, but we are held responsible for what we do with our lives – whether our nature has excessive control over us and we are its slaves, or whether we can occasionally master it and, to some extent and to the best of our ability, reduce the incidence of temptation and sin in our lives. So we take comfort from the Lord Jesus Christ.

Yet Jesus also had this same nature and a heart that could have deceived him had it not been restrained and contained. He knew what was in man and all the forces, passions and pleasures of a man; he knew what

23

material possessions were and how they could make life more comfortable. He knew the pride and egotism of self and the havoc it could wreak, if it was allowed to vaunt itself and become puffed up. He was not exempt from any of these forces which are common to man. He suffered acutely in overcoming both temptation and sin. Wondrously he was not "drawn away ... and enticed", as James describes it. He focused his mind on God. He wrestled with the forces, passions, desires and lusts, and rejected them. He would not be drawn into carnal ways or carnal thoughts. He quickly recognised the diabolical voice that was provoking him to be his adversary and his enemy. He overcame it totally; he did not sin.

But the pattern of temptation when it presented itself would have been the same for Jesus as it is for us. He was not excused the process even though he was exceptional in its repudiation. This is why we can exclaim with the apostle:

"O wretched man that I am! who shall deliver me from the body of this death? I thank God through Jesus Christ our Lord." (Romans 7:24,25)

24

3

FULFILLING ALL RIGHTEOUSNESS

IN view of what we have discovered about the horror of human nature and the deceitful human mind and forces of desire, it was vitally important that Jesus sought out and totally relied upon a power and strength far in excess of any opposing force he was likely to face in his ministry of redemption. This was particularly important in the wilderness experience which immediately followed his baptism. For here he was alone, separated from all human companionship and support. His forerunner had baptized him, and would declare that Jesus was the "Lamb of God, which taketh away the sin of the world", and would increase, whilst John himself would decrease. John the Baptist would have been a delightful companion and a source of strength during Jesus' forty days and nights in the wilderness had they been together; but he was in other places, 'preparing the way of the Lord, and making his paths straight'. Jesus was alone. Where and what would be the source of his resolve and strength?

"It is written"

This was an important phrase in the vocabulary of Jesus. Across the four Gospels he is recorded as using it on twenty-five occasions. Some of these are duplicated as the following table shows.

Circumstances used	Gospel references
The temptations – 6 references with 3 each in Matthew and Luke	Matthew 4:4,7,10 & Luke 4:4,8,12

John the Baptist – 3 references	Matthew 11:10; Mark 9:13 & Luke 7:27
His own ministry – 5 references	Mark 7:6; John 6:45; 8:17; 10:34 & 15:25
The temple – 3 references	Matthew 21:13; Mark 11:17 & Luke 19:46
His own sacrifice – 7 references	Matthew 26:31; Mark 9:12; 14:21; 14:27; Luke 20:17,18; 22:37; 24:46
Betrayal – 1 reference	Matthew 26:24

In using the phrase, Jesus quoted from or alluded to the Old Testament as follows:

Scriptures	Comments
Deuteronomy (4 references) 8:3; 6:13 & 6:16 Deuteronomy 17:6	First 3 references are in Matthew 4:4,7,10 & Luke 4:4,8,12; fourth in John 8:17
Malachi 3:1	Used twice in Matthew 11:10 & Luke 7:27
Psalms (7 references) 41:9; 55:12,13; 69:4; 82:6; 88:18; 109:6-16 & 118:22	Matthew 26:24; Mark 14:21; Luke 20:17; John 10:34; 15:25
Isaiah (5 references) 8:14; 29:13; 53:12; 54:13 & 56:7	Matthew 21:13; Mark 7:6, 11:17; Luke 19:46; 20:18; 22:37; John 6:45 4th ref. used 3 times

26

Jeremiah 7:11	Used 3 times in Matthew 21:13; Mark 11:17; Luke 19:46
Daniel 2:45	Luke 20:18
Zechariah 13:7	Used 3 times in Matthew 26:31; Mark 9:13, 14:27
References to 'Law, Psalms & Prophets' hinting at: Psalm 22:6; Isaiah 53:2,3; Daniel 2:35; 9:26; Zechariah 13:7	Mark 9:12; 14:21; Luke 24:46

The baptism of Jesus

"Then cometh Jesus from Galilee to Jordan unto John, to be baptized of him. But John forbad him, saying, I have need to be baptized of thee, and comest thou to me? And Jesus answering said unto him, Suffer it to be so now: for thus it becometh us to fulfil all righteousness. Then he suffered him. And Jesus, when he was baptized, went up straightway out of the water: and, lo, the heavens were opened unto him, and he saw the Spirit of God descending like a dove, and lighting upon him: and lo a voice from heaven, saying, This is my beloved Son, in whom I am well pleased." (Matthew 3:13-17)

The critical time in the life of Jesus began at his baptism. It is true that the previous thirty years had also been a time of testing and evaluation, but now it all crystallised at his baptism: the Lord had embarked upon the work of redemption, "I delight to do thy will, O my God: yea, thy law is within my heart". He knew the outcome would be his death by crucifixion, and Daniel's prophecy had already predetermined when that took

27

place. But first, he needed to commence his public ministry to appeal to his people and to turn them back to God, so he faithfully submitted to baptism to fulfil all righteousness. He knew also that his ministry would bring him into direct conflict with the spiritual leaders of the nation, who would engineer his death, but such a course could not begin until he publicly declared himself by his baptism, so:

"Jesus answering said unto him, Suffer it to be so now: for thus it becometh us to fulfil all righteousness." (Matthew 3:15)

What does his baptism mean? The following list demonstrates the breadth of meaning:

- He acknowledged the total supremacy of God as the Judge of all the earth to do right.
- The righteousness of God required the death of all Adam's descendants because of the disobedience in Eden.
- As Jesus was born in Adam he shared the same mortal nature as all his fellows and this had to die – but he was personally sinless.
- He accepted that all human nature was corruptible because of its inclination to evil and that he too would die.
- He declared the righteousness of God by being baptized.
- He entered into his covenant with God by his baptism.
- He demonstrated humility when he accepted God's command of baptism which led inevitably to the cross.
- He suppressed the temptation to reject baptism by presenting himself as 'holier than thou' – as he was in his personal life but not by nature.
- His baptism resulted in a public declaration that he was both Messiah and Son of God.

- John the Baptist was a witness and forerunner of the work of Christ – "thus it *becometh us* to fulfil all righteousness".

- Baptism was the sign of his voluntary intention to embark on the ministry as the appointed Redeemer.

- Baptism was his willingness to please his Father in everything he did and said, even though it was through self-denial and the hurt it brought upon himself, because he loved his Father and would honour Him.

"And lo a voice from heaven, saying, This is my beloved Son, in whom I am well pleased."

(Matthew 3:17)

This was the positive declaration of the Father's approval of what Jesus had just done and would do in the ministry. Here also was an affirmation of his Sonship and his relationship with heaven. There could be no doubt, either in the mind of Jesus or by those who heard the same voice that he was the beloved Son. Here was the seed of the woman, the Prophet like unto Moses, the long promised Messiah, the future King, the Son of God, the Saviour. The responsibility lay heavily on the shoulders of Jesus. It was his alone. Could he face all the challenges and temptations that the future would bring? There was always the danger that nothing was sure until the purpose was finally accomplished and all temptations were put behind him and defeated. Would he be able to overcome them when tested, and be a proven servant, one in whom the Father, in the fullness of joy, could delight?

Into the wilderness

"Jesus was led up of the Spirit into the wilderness."

(Matthew 4:1)

"And immediately the Spirit driveth him forth into the wilderness." (Mark 1:12, RV)

"Jesus was led by the Spirit in the wilderness during the forty days." (Luke 4:1, RV)

Two interesting points emerge from these three references. Mark writes, "the Spirit driveth": this suggests reluctance by Jesus to go knowing what would befall him.

Luke writes, "led by the Spirit during forty days". This implies an ever present nearness of the Spirit during the wilderness experience. What is this? Precisely what form did the leading of the Spirit take?

Is this the Holy Spirit providing some guidance? It has been suggested. The three references above illustrate one of the earliest conflicts faced by Jesus, because he was both Son of God and born of a woman into the human condition. Knowing the trials and difficulties that would befall him at the end of the ministry, and perhaps wondering whether he could physically and emotionally endure them, he would naturally be reluctant to venture into the wilderness. At the same time, the power of the voice from heaven, his baptismal vow, and the declaration of his Father's pleasure in him, would be the urgent encouragement to proceed. He knew what he ought to do, and why he was sent; and this spirit of knowledge and the fear of the Lord, this wisdom and understanding of the desperate plight of his fellow men who needed to be freed from the bondage of sin and death, were able to overcome any natural hesitation which was present. The motivation to go forward came from within. It was his spirit of love and co-operation with the Father which was the driver. It had to be, otherwise his service and faith could not have been willing and voluntary.

The Authorised Version of the Luke passage can be read to support a view that the three recorded temptations were repeated during the forty days, but it is worth considering that they were deferred until the end of that period. Mark and Luke in fact tell us that temptations of one kind or another occurred, as it would be most unlikely that the forty days and nights would be totally temptation free, given the nature of Jesus in the days of his flesh, with the three wilderness temptations only coming in full force at the end of the six weeks when the Lord was physically weak.

The divine records move on immediately to the end of the forty days to describe the next stage, after this lonely six-week vigil of Jesus, wrestling with many temptations:

"When he had fasted forty days and forty nights, he afterward hungered." (Matthew 4:2, RV)

"He was in the wilderness forty days tempted of Satan; and he was with the wild beasts; and the angels ministered unto him." (Mark 1:13, RV)

"He did eat nothing in those days: and when they were completed, he hungered." (Luke 4:2, RV)

Both Matthew and Luke answer the question, 'When did the three recorded temptations take place?' Their answer is: 'At the end of forty days'. However it must be accepted that Jesus would get hungry well before the forty days were ended. This would most likely be at the end of the first day and certainly by the second or third days. Also, temptations of differing subtleties and kinds would have to be battled with, from the moment of his baptism until he got into the wilderness – perhaps while he was being driven there by the Spirit.

Maybe we imagine Jesus striding out purposefully, head held high, arms swinging at his sides, keeping up a regular and rhythmic pace as he walked into the wilderness. Would he not be a thoughtful and prayerful man with great purpose and resolve in his heart as he journeyed alone into those lonely desert places? He knew he was to face a severe trial of his own will, and of his determination to fulfil the righteousness of God and honour the voice from heaven which had so recently approved of him and his dedication at baptism.

Mark tells us about the "wild beasts" which were in the wilderness with him. Why should he record this? He might just be describing the physical dangers of "the waste howling wilderness", but more likely he intended to take his readers back into the Old Testament, and

31

two passages of scripture in particular. The first is from Deuteronomy 8:

> "... who led thee through that great and terrible wilderness, wherein were fiery serpents, and scorpions, and drought, where there was no water; who brought thee forth water out of the rock of flint; who fed thee in the wilderness with manna, which thy fathers knew not, that he might humble thee, and that he might prove thee, to do thee good at thy latter end."   (verses 15,16)

Moses reminds the Children of Israel about the extreme hardships of their wilderness journey; also how God had looked after them with gifts they "knew not". In Deuteronomy 8 is found the answer to the first temptation of turning stones into bread. The wilderness was the dwelling-place of the Israel called out of Egypt, whose experiences were to be the same as the second Son also called out of Egypt. That he was not harmed indicated God's care and protection, despite the "wild beasts".

The second passage from the Old Testament is Psalm 91:

> "Thou shalt tread upon the lion and adder: the young lion and the dragon shalt thou trample under feet."   (verse 13)

Given the context of this verse – that it's used as part of the Lord's defence against the subtle invitation to engage the angelic services for personal protection, and a display of spectacular heroics – we may take the reference to dangerous and wild animals as being literal in the first place. But the Psalmist is taking us both backwards and forwards in thought and understanding. For this is a reference to the overcoming by Jesus of the serpent power of sin; and to the curse imposed in Eden being lifted because of his triumph over sin, beginning with the three temptations he conquered. He was continuously triumphant in similar stressful situations as his ministry progressed. As angels closed up the open mouths of the lions when Daniel was in their den, so

Mark is hinting that because of Jesus' victory over the sin power in the wilderness, the "wild beasts" lost their natural ferocity, and were 'tamed' by the presence of the conquering Son. This is a cameo of the kingdom of God, fulfilling Isaiah 11:6-9, Genesis 3:15 and Psalm 8:6-8; also Isaiah 35:1,2,7-9, that the person and the power of the King had caused the wilderness to blossom as the rose in millennial glory.

How did Jesus respond during the forty days?

This is not recorded in the Gospel narratives of the wilderness temptations, but he would have been totally triumphant. He would have resorted to much prayer. He knew his Bible inside out even though it's doubtful he would have had a scroll with him. He would be able to recall the scripture perfectly from his memory. By the time the forty days were ended, he knew by this experience "that man doth not live by bread only, but by every word that proceedeth out of the mouth of the LORD". He had proved it.

How did he stave off his hunger and thirst? There is no record of either food or water being provided during the forty days. In fact Matthew tells us that he "fasted forty days and forty nights, and afterwards he hungered". There have been examples (even in our times) of great weakness and illness which follow a prolonged period of sustained starvation, even when forcibly made to drink water. How many times had the thought to provide some food and drink been in Jesus' mind, especially given the strongest hints in Deuteronomy 8:15,16? Often, we suspect. Would it have been sinful to satisfy the hunger pangs? After all, God created the hunger sensation, so we can take food to sustain ourselves and live healthily and happily. Hunger, although natural, is not sinful, so to satisfy it is not sinful. We give thanks to God to sanctify His gift of our meals. But the means employed to supply the necessary food and drink would have provided the trial for Jesus. What could Jesus have eaten to satisfy his natural needs? Is the pattern set by John the Baptist helpful?

The following quotation may be of interest:

"In the gospels ... locusts are never mentioned as devastating insects. In Matthew 3:4 and in the parallel passage in Mark 1:6 they appear only as an article of *food*. It is in this character, then, that we have chiefly to study them here. The word used [for locusts] is *akris*; it is said that John the Baptist fed on 'locusts and wild honey'. An ancient tradition of the Christian Church held that the locusts eaten by the Baptist were not insects, but the pods or husks of a tree, the carob or locust tree (*Ceratonia siliqua*, Arab. *kharrûb*). Curiously enough, this old interpretation has been resuscitated in our own times by Cheyne (Encyc. Bibl. ii. cols. 2136, 2499), who sees in the locusts of John the Baptist 'carob-beans', but for reasons which do not seem to us convincing. In fact, locusts are a well known food in Eastern countries ... The Law of Israel, which strictly forbade the eating of creeping things, insects, etc., made an exception in the case of locusts ...[1]

The above article goes on to explain quite graphically that locusts (the insects) being food, are caught, prepared, cooked and eaten particularly by desert dwellers and nomads, such as the Bedouin, with some locusts offered for sale in Middle Eastern markets. The following two short articles taken from the web provide confirmation:

"This view is supported by some Bible dictionaries and other references which tell of an Arab stew made from the locust bug that is a pest to crops. Both Vine and Strong write about roasted locusts with the head, wings and legs removed. They were salted and also cooked with butter. In other New Testament uses of *akris*, the pest is clearly implied, *not* the tree."[2]

"While the consumption of insect locusts was not completely unheard of, it was most uncommon and highly unusual, relegated to last ditch options in

---

1 See Leviticus 11:22 – Quotation from Hastings, *Dictionary of Christ and the Gospels,* 1913 reprint, article "Locusts in the Gospels", Volume 2, pages 44,45.
2 www.geocities.com/athens/Parthenon/3664/locusts.html.

stark survival situations. John the Baptist could have eaten those bugs in their short season. It is quite possible that the events surrounding the references in Matthew and Mark coincided with the short season, when grasshopper-like locusts were available, providing John with a high protein sustenance as many adult and larval insects are a source of 'survival-chow'."[3]

But by far the weight of current evidence is that John the Baptist survived on the edible fruit of the locust tree, and not by eating bugs, adult locusts, the flying grasshopper-like insects. The tree flowers between August and November. Winifred Walker in *All the Plants of the Bible,* writes about the fruit of the carob or locust tree that it is "accepted in the East as the food on which John the Baptist fed ... it is native to the eastern Mediterranean region".

Here are three more references which support the view that John the Baptist ate the pods taken from the carob tree:

"The Carob is a leguminous evergreen tree [*Ceratonia Siliqua*] native to the E. Mediterranean region and cultivated elsewhere. It is sometimes known as locust, or 'St. John's Bread', in the belief that 'the locusts' on which John fed were carob pods. The tree, about 50 feet (15m) tall, bears compound, glossy leaves with thick leaflets. Its red flowers are followed by flat, leathery pods that contain 5-15 hard brown seeds embedded in a sweet edible pulp that tastes similar to chocolate."[4]

"*Ceratonia Siliqua*, Carob, is often called the poor man's bread and it's regarded as a symbol of humility. The Carob tree or Locust [the husks of which were fed to the swine – Luke 15:16] is also known as St. John's Bread [Mark 1:6]. John the Baptist sustained himself on the Carob beans, otherwise known as Locust Beans, while travelling in the wilderness. It is well

3   www.antipas.net/14faq.htm
4   *The Columbia Encyclopedia*, 6th edition.

35

known that in Biblical times wild [non-cultivated] carobs were in abundance and are not mentioned in the Old Testament; its Hebrew name *'haruv'* often appears in the Mishnah and the Talmud."[5]

Marshall's Bible Handbook[6], in the section on "The Animals and Insects of Palestine", after referring to the Mosaic Law as allowing the Hebrews to eat locusts, also makes reference to some scholars who "think that John the Baptist's food was not the locust, but the fruit of the carob tree – 'husks' much like the prodigal son ate (Mark 1:6, Luke 15:16)".

It is quite probable then that John the Baptist ate 'locust beans' from the carob tree and wild honey during his time in the wilderness. He could simply pick the beans and the honey off the trees. Would it have been possible for Jesus to have picked both beans and honey from off the trees, given that he might have been in the same general area as the Baptist was earlier and such trees were growing and fruiting there? To 'glean' the tree is one thing, but specifically and selfishly to use God's Holy Spirit to satisfy personal needs, although they were urgent and even honourable, is quite another. Yet Jesus did neither. He would depend on his Father to sustain his life. It is written, "Man shall not live by bread alone".

---

5 http://www.flowersinisrael.com/ceratoniasiliqua_page.htm
6 First published edition 1980 by Thomas Nelson, page 244.

4

IT IS WRITTEN

THE Book of Deuteronomy and the retelling of the history of the Children of Israel, confirming the faithfulness and activity of God, was Jesus' guidebook so far as the wilderness temptations were concerned. It was to Deuteronomy that he appealed on each of the three recorded occasions, to find the counter-argument to defeat the tempter. There is no reason to doubt that he referred to this same book of Moses when temptations occurred again during the ministry. Although Jesus 'quoted' from what we know as Deuteronomy chapters 6 and 8 to resist those diabolical suggestions, it is the early chapters of Deuteronomy that provide the wider context of Jesus' victory. What Moses recorded about God's dealings with the Children of Israel, emphasising God's faithfulness and the greatness of His promises and covenant making, was the basis on which Jesus secured his own victory. What had happened to the chosen people who were brought up out of the land of Egypt and from the house of bondage, was a foreshadowing of the life and experiences of the later born Son of promise who was also called out of Egypt.

A schedule of instructions, commandments and statutes had been revealed for acceptance by and understanding of the Children of Israel, and when practised would be for their long term, as well as their immediate benefit. Although a favourable response was hoped for, it was not generally forthcoming and the people deteriorated in their worship and behaviour before God. They lost the promised benefits of the covenant, and forfeited their inheritance and long life in the land. These same instructions, commandments and statutes, should have been accepted and practised by every individual member of the nation, if they were to be effective and beneficial for the whole. The nation could only be improved when individuals accepted their personal responsibility in this matter. The same is true of the ecclesia, with the personal responsibility of each contributing to the well-being of the One Body as a whole. When slackness happens in any department, the whole Body begins to break down. This was equally true for Jesus. The royal and divine law would prosper the way of those who accepted it and Jesus knew this. The law was from his Father, and because he was a faithful Son, he would honour and perform it. He knew it was helpful and right.

Moses knew, however, that the nature of the people as well as his own was flawed. He had revealed this in his own conduct and had personally suffered. It had cost him his entry into the promised land. This flawed nature was inclined to rebellion. So Moses emphasised the message, in the retelling of all their ways, by prefacing his instruction with the words, "Hear, O Israel". It was a call to action, to reformation, to faith, to dependency on God. It was a call to listen and do, and subsequently to heed the message, for "it is written". Most importantly, it was a call to honour God and magnify Him in every aspect of daily life. It should have regulated personal conduct, neighbour to neighbour, the individual to God, as well as within the family and Israel's relationship with surrounding nations.

"Now therefore hearken, O Israel, unto the statutes and unto the judgments, which I teach you, for to do them, that ye may live, and go in and possess the land which the LORD God of your fathers giveth you." (Deuteronomy 4:1)

"And Moses called all Israel, and said unto them, Hear, O Israel, the statutes and judgments which I speak in your ears this day, that ye may learn them, and keep, and do them." (5:1)

If we ask, 'Why should Israel hear, learn, keep and do them?', the answer is: they were the covenant people and this was their part of the agreement, but also because they were on the border of the land promised to the fathers to "go in and possess" it for an inheritance.

There is a minimum of thirty-three references in Deuteronomy chapters 3-12 to 'possessing the land', as the following two tables show. As an example, "He brought us out from thence [Egypt] that he might bring us in, to give us the land which he sware unto our fathers" (6:23). This was the encouragement, both individually and nationally.

"Go in to possess the land"

Ref.	Brief paraphrase
3:18	God has given you this land to possess it.
4:1	Go in and possess the land which the Lord gives you.
4:5	The land where you go to possess it.
4:14	Do them in the land you go over to possess.
4:22	You shall go over and possess that good land.
4:26	The land you go over Jordan to possess.
5:31	They may do them in the land which I give them to possess.
5:33	Prolong your days in the land which you shall possess.
6:1	Do them in the land you go to possess.
6:18	Go in and possess the good land.
7:1	God shall bring you into the land you go to possess.
8:1	Go in and possess the land.

9:1	Pass over Jordan this day, to go in to possess nations.
9:4	The Lord has brought me in to possess this land.
9:5	Go to possess their land.
9:6	God does not give you this land to possess for your righteousness.
9:23	Go up and possess the land which I have given you.
10:11	They may go in and possess the land which I swore to give them.
11:8	Be strong and go in and possess the land.
11:10	The land you go in to possess is not as Egypt.
11:11	But the land you go to possess drinks the rain of heaven.
11:29	The land you go to possess.
11:31	Pass over Jordan to go in to possess the land which the Lord gives you.
12:1	The land the Lord gives you to possess all your days.
12:29	The Lord cuts off the nations you go to possess.

Supplementary list

4:21	That good land the Lord gives you for an inheritance.
4:38	The Lord will bring you in to give you their land for an inheritance.
5:16	Your days may be prolonged in the land the Lord gives you.

6:3	The Lord promised you the land which flows with milk and honey.
6:10	God shall have brought you into the land he swore to our fathers.
6:23	He brought us out of Egypt to bring us in, to give us the land he swore to our fathers.
7:13	Blessings in the land he swore to our fathers to give you.
11:23	You shall possess greater nations and mightier than yourselves.

Exhortation from Deuteronomy

There was plenty of exhortation in the early Deuteronomy chapters for Jesus. In chapter 4, for example, there is a powerful lesson about the events at Sinai (verses 10-24). From verses 29-40 there is a section which could be paraphrased as, 'What to do in difficult circumstances', or 'How to recover if you are in danger of slipping'. The answer is, 'Remember God, even in your extremity, and consider again His faithfulness and trustworthiness, His nearness and willingness to help, and His readiness to respond to your cries'. It was the same for Jesus during his ministry; never easy, and always fraught with difficulty and opposition. Yet Jesus never forgot the source of his strength.

Consider these verses in the light of the temptations:

"But if from thence thou shalt seek the LORD thy God, thou shalt find him, if thou seek him with all thy heart and with all thy soul. When thou art in tribulation, and all these things are come upon thee, even in the latter days, if thou turn to the LORD thy God, and shalt be obedient to his voice; (for the LORD thy God is a merciful God;) he will not forsake thee, neither destroy thee, nor forget the covenant of thy fathers which he sware unto them." (verses 29-31)

The temptation to do whatever possible wrong the voice in his head suggested, needed to be silenced by the

41

greater and precious promises of support from heaven. There were two voices sounding, creating a conflict and each making an appeal for obedience – the diabolical earthly voice and the holy divine voice. One offered self-gratification, however innocent, by turning stones into bread and he could have it now. The other promised victory and eternal things, but not yet. Those times and seasons had been put into the Father's power. He would have been in constant tribulation in the wilderness for forty days and nights, for each moment of each hour of each day of the six weeks. But in the law of the Lord he could find what to do: "Turn to the LORD thy God, and ... be obedient unto his voice" (4:30). The assurance was, "He will not forsake thee, neither destroy thee, nor forget the covenant of thy fathers which he sware unto them" (verse 31).

Here is another exhortation:

> "Out of heaven he made thee to hear his voice, that he might instruct thee: and upon earth he shewed thee his great fire." (verse 36)

Jesus did hear the voice out of heaven on the day of his baptism. He had been instructed. He had known of great things on the earth, the people's Egyptian bondage, their freedom and continuing and difficult existence. But he also knew in his day his own people's Roman bondage, their need for freedom, not from Rome although that would have been beneficial for them, but more importantly freedom from the great enemy of sin. He was aware of his own miraculous birth, his possession of the Holy Spirit, and he had already heard the voice from heaven once. The witness had been made. What was needed now was to prove and then believe that these things were as true in his own daily experience as they had been in the days of Moses and Israel in the wilderness.

> "Thou shalt keep therefore his statutes, and his commandments, which I command thee this day, that it may go well with thee, and with thy children after thee, and that thou mayest prolong thy days upon the earth,

which the LORD thy God giveth thee, for ever."
(verse 40)

Given that the experiences of the children of Israel, both in the wilderness and the faithful years in the land, are a pattern of the life of the Lord Jesus, this passage could well be a reference to his ministry and the promise of 'success' in his preaching campaigns based on the law of his Father, when once he had a positive response from his hearers. We have a reference to the disciples and believers of all ages ("thy children after thee") and the kingdom of God in which the Father will "prolong thy days upon the earth for ever". How very appropriate.

"And Moses called all Israel, and said unto them, Hear, O Israel, the statutes and judgments which I speak in your ears this day, that ye may learn them, and keep, and do them. The LORD our God made a covenant with us in Horeb. The LORD made not this covenant with our fathers, but with us, who are all of us here alive this day."
(5:1-3)

The Sinai covenant was actually made with the fathers or the grandparents of that generation to whom Moses was speaking, but they had died in the wilderness. The verses show how the covenant is held to be made with each succeeding generation, for Moses said twice, "made a covenant with us". This personal involvement of every member of the nation entering the covenant bond is emphasised again in Deuteronomy 29:10-15. This time Moses added the words, "also with him that is not here with us this day". This may refer to those temporarily absent, but also indicates that the same covenant is made with the generations to come. This means the covenant was made personally with Jesus – it was for him to observe and keep and do, because he was "alive this day".

Listening to the voice

As in our day when there are so many voices clamouring for attention, so it was in Jesus' day. It was important he heard the right voice to overcome the power of sin.

He had to believe the voice which came with authority to confirm his life's objectives. This determination was set in motion from the earliest recorded event at the age of twelve in the temple with the doctors of the law. But resolve at twelve years old needed to be renewed, not just once a year at Passover, but daily, given the flawed nature which Jesus shared. His heart and mind had to be sharply focused on the cross. So he listened to the divine voice and its emphasis. This is why it's instructive to consider the early chapters of Deuteronomy to see how they could have been helpful to the Lord Jesus Christ in his wilderness times. This was the teaching he had to heed, for "it is written". The following five examples are suggested as possibilities. There will be others.

> "And in the wilderness, where thou hast seen how that the LORD thy God bare thee, as a man doth bear his son, in all the way that ye went, until ye came into this place."   (Deuteronomy 1:31)

This would be powerful and faith strengthening. Here is the reassurance. At the end of his experiences Jesus had successfully survived the forty days and nights. He had been borne along as a Son, as he went to and fro through the waste howling wilderness. He would realise he had been looked after and protected, even from wild beasts. He had been heard when he had prayed in this lonely place. There are textual links with Psalm 91:11,12 which formed part of his triumphant defence against the 'pinnacle of the temple' temptation. These links are in the words "shall bear thee up" and "keep thee in all thy ways", from the Psalm, corresponding with "bare thee" and "in all the way", in the Deuteronomy reference above. But that practical assurance had already been given here. What God had promised to do for his first-born son out of Egypt, he promised for his Spirit-born Son of promise. The difference was that the natural first-born had rebelled. The second Son believed the voice and found it to be true. He knew God would be faithful and keep his word because "it is written".

> "For the LORD thy God hath blessed thee in all the works of thy hand: he knoweth thy walking through

44

this great wilderness: these forty years [days] the LORD thy God hath been with thee; thou hast lacked nothing." (Deuteronomy 2:7)

Jesus would believe his wilderness circumstances were known by the Lord his God, his Father. After forty desperate days and nights of resisting devilish voices, and being challenged by the ability to accomplish whatever he wanted to, he knew he lacked nothing of real eternal value and hope. Not one of the promises of God and covenant conditions had 'fallen to the ground'. We can perhaps see a tenuous link with the 'stones into bread' temptation. On behalf of the Children of Israel the angel provided manna on a daily basis, and then confirmed, "Man doth not live by bread only, but by every word that proceedeth out of the mouth of the LORD". In Jesus' time the stones remained on the ground. As far as we know, he did not pick them up even remotely to consider their change into bread. No fragment of bread fell to the ground as 'leftovers' or waste. He was no doubt weary and worn after the forty-day vigil and contemplation. He truly understood the meaning of the baptismal declaration, "Thou art my beloved Son", and concluded 'he lacked nothing'.

"This day will I begin to put the dread of thee and the fear of thee upon the nations that are under the whole heaven, who shall hear report of thee, and shall tremble, and be in anguish because of thee." (Deuteronomy 2:25)

From the wilderness of temptation Jesus went into Galilee to commence his public ministry. But it was not with "dread" and "fear" that the people and nations heard, although they will at his second coming, but rather with awe and wonder because of his teaching and miracles. The power of the Lord's preaching, the consistency of the message, the call to repentance and the offer of redemption from sin, caused the people to "hear him gladly"; to say "never man spake like this man", for he spoke "as one having authority, and not as the scribes". But he was the Word made flesh, and had a glory which declared him to be the only begotten of the Father, full of grace and truth. His message of redemption was to call men and women to know God, to love God and honour Him, for "It is written in the prophets, And they shall be all taught of God". God's activity in drawing men and women to salvation was made clear by his preaching and in the process of them coming to Jesus as the Saviour (John 6:44,45). He presented a powerful challenge to the people of his day to 'let go and let God' into their lives, in a way they had not previously known and sadly had never been taught. False teaching and men's traditions, even that of the elders, was to be put aside and rejected. Instead, "it is written, Thou shalt worship the Lord thy God, and him only shalt thou serve". Lip service was not good enough. Commitment of the life was required. The people heard the reports, and began to see and learn the power of the Gospel. But the time would come to ask, as the prophet had indicated, "Who has believed our report?" even though "the arm of the LORD" had been revealed (Isaiah 53:1), and then the cross would be carried. But for the moment, "This day will I begin to ..." was his Father's assurance.

> "And I besought the LORD at that time, saying, O Lord GOD, thou hast begun to show thy servant thy greatness, and thy mighty hand: for what God is there in heaven or in earth, that can do according to thy works, and according to thy might?"
>
> (Deuteronomy 3:23,24)

This was Moses' prayer that he should be allowed to enter the land, but how appropriate are these words in the heart of Jesus at the end of the temptations, when the devil left him for a season. His wilderness experience had reinforced, if this was necessary, that the Lord his God was his Father, his One Lord. With whom could he be compared? He had learned again God's mighty hand, for angels came and ministered to him when the devil left him. He had been safe even among the wild beasts. It's as if Jesus was praying about his own triumphant situation and thanking his Father for the victory, for these are the sentiments of Moses to Joshua, even his Jesus, as is recorded just two to three verses earlier:

"And I commanded Joshua at that time, saying, Thine eyes have seen all that the LORD your God hath done unto these two kings: so shall the LORD do unto all the kingdoms whither thou passest. Ye shall not fear them: for the LORD your God he shall fight for you." (verses 21,22)

As there was evidence of the work of God amongst the Children of Israel in their wilderness ministry, so there was in Jesus' life also. In Jesus' wilderness experience the two kings would be represented firstly by the wild beasts as a real physical presence, and secondly by the devil as the tempter, the sin power. These verses remind us of what happened before the Children of Israel entered the promised land. The two kings, Og of Bashan and Sihon of the Amorites, operated in the territory which proved to be the final stages of the wilderness journey – the biggest test came at the end from the strongest and most implacable enemies. They opposed the Children of Israel and refused them easy passage to the land to possess it. Battles took place and the two kings were defeated.

So it was in the life of Jesus before he commenced his ministry in the promised land. At the end of forty days of loneliness, hunger and repudiating temptation and trials, the Gospels tell us that the Lord's severest test came from the strongest enemy – the implacable evil one, the devil. The tempter met him head on and the battle for supremacy was played out. But this was no game, as it was fought against the backdrop of salvation for those of the human race who were prepared to believe the Lord's claims, or they would face everlasting oblivion. But Jesus knew that "it is written" and the battle was won. Both representative kings were overcome and Jesus was victorious, as he would be again in his coming future kingdom. Similar things would be accomplished for various people during his earthly ministry when bodies were healed, eyes made to see, ears were opened, leprosy was cured, the lame made to walk and run, and the mentally disabled restored to their right minds. The sin power which wielded such evil and havoc and came in such hideous forms would be conquered again. The reassurance is given in verse 22, "Ye shall not fear them: for the LORD your God he shall fight for you". The power of God would be in evidence again.

These five examples given above show how the early chapters of Deuteronomy could have provided help to Jesus during his forty days wilderness period, as chapters 6 and 8 did in the triumphant victory over the three specific and recorded temptations. It would be strange indeed if no reference whatsoever was made to the earlier exhortations and warnings of Moses, to refute those trials which he faced during the six-week period – especially as Moses was retelling the historical experiences of the Children of Israel, and when Jesus lifted out three other significant portions from these same early parts of Deuteronomy in the defeat of the tempter. There is no mention in the temptation accounts in the Gospels to quotations from these early Deuteronomy chapters. Likewise, there is no record of any other specific trials apart from the reference in Luke 4:2, "being forty days tempted of the devil". But we need to bear in mind that hunger, the declaration that he was the Son of God with angelic care, the equally certain assurances from the prophets, and Jesus being the designated King of the world, would all present daily challenges which needed putting away and rejecting. This would take a resolute will and a strong faith, to be reinforced and encouraged by mental reminders and reflections on the word of the Lord, especially those specific portions of Deuteronomy which had to do with their fathers' wilderness wanderings.

The practice of the precept

We now consider Deuteronomy 6:4-9. The way described is high and holy, with personal responsibility being emphasised:

"Hear, O Israel: The LORD our God is one LORD: and thou shalt love the LORD thy God with all thine heart, and with all thy soul, and with all thy might. And these words, which I command thee this day, shall be in thine heart: and thou shalt teach them diligently unto thy children, and shalt talk of them when thou sittest in thine house, and when thou walkest by the way, and when thou liest down, and when thou risest up. And thou shalt bind them for a sign upon thine hand, and they shall be as frontlets between thine eyes. And thou shalt write them upon the posts of thy house, and on thy gates." (6:4-9)

Here is sound advice to keep instruction alive and in all the circumstances of the disciples' life – both day and night, in all generations. The way to reinforce this is to talk about the Truth. It is all based on verse 4, "The LORD our God is One LORD". This doctrine underscores the unity of thought, action, and the focus for life. It means no counter attractions or challenges to God should be introduced. The worship and honour of the One Lord is demanded of us all, from heart, soul, strength and mind. Anything less, anything different, breaches the doctrine of the One Lord, and dishonours Him because of other gods and other interests. These things introduce rivals into the life of the disciple and this is called idolatry.

This was the reason why God through Moses emphasised the principle of separation from surrounding Gentile nations. The Children of Israel were to keep away from obvious dangers and reduce the opportunity for temptation. They were to be holy in their living – giving God the glory, practising personal self-denial, because the promise and the covenant were mighty, glorious and generous.

For Jesus the principle was, "It is written". It should be for us as well.

5

THE TEACHING OF JESUS ABOUT TEMPTATION

"Jesus did not commit himself unto them, because he knew all men, and needed not that any should testify of man: for he knew what was in man."

(John 2:24,25)

JESUS knew what was in man. How did he know? Was it some form of sixth sense, a telepathy which provided this knowledge? Was it by the power of Spirit, or similar to the way he read men's thoughts and hearts even before the words were spoken out loud, much to the consternation of others? Or was it by his own experience of the ways of the world; or because he was a man and knew his own self? The verses above are speaking about the human nature which Jesus shared. He had personally experienced and been tempted in the same way as all men and women. So he knew what was in man, because of his own powerful sensations. He knew the process of enticement and the thinking of human minds. He knew the deviousness of human hearts. He knew it because his own heart tried to take him there. He had experienced the process; he had wrestled with the problems, and he came out victorious.

Because he was a man, he knew how a man thought, processed information, reacted to situations. He also knew how much strength and will was needed to overcome his temptations. He humbly realised, like everybody else, that it was "not in man that walketh to direct his steps", but unlike everybody else, he and only he, was the Son of God. It meant that Jesus' personal knowledge of human nature governed his relationship with his fellows, because he knew all the limitations, weaknesses and lack of resistance. But it also governed his relationship with his Father, for he knew that here was the only source of comfort and strength which would assist him to overcome the temptations and maintain his faith, and so fulfil his work as the Redeemer.

The wilderness testing was not the only period of trial in his life. The three temptations were the climax of the forty days in the wilderness. They were typical of what Jesus endured during the forty days for (as discussed earlier) there would have been some kind of temptation ongoing during the length of the wilderness period. The three recorded events might have been the severest tests he endured, and therefore selected by the Gospel writers to demonstrate that Jesus experienced the worst there was. He was tempted in all points, and none of us can say we suffer something the Lord did not. As we agonise because of the tests of our faith, integrity and loyalty, so did he. The same serpentine forces and diabolical impulses that frustrate us also tempted him to follow his own inclinations – except he did not follow them. He was in total control of himself, and marvellously overcame them. He could do this because he was the Son of God, but also because he knew what was in man. Moreover he constantly remembered what was in man, and to that extent was prepared for the conflict when the impulses came to him.

The Lord's Prayer

Jesus makes his first recorded public reference to temptation in what we know as the Lord's Prayer in Matthew 6:9-13. It was not to be the last time in the ministry that he referred to it. His whole life was plagued by it and everyday was a conflict to overcome the fleshly forces. He needed to turn away from temptation to prevent himself being drawn away by his own lust, for that would bring forth sin. Jesus uses the word 'temptation' another five times, and three of these are locked together at the end of the ministry, just before and during the time he spends in the Garden of Gethsemane. These three references all come in Luke. We shall examine them.

Self-confidence

"And lead us not into temptation, but deliver us
from evil."   (Matthew 6:13)

For those who are children in spiritual things, the
babes of the family and the lambs of the flock, and who
seem to ooze confidence in their own abilities to combat
unhelpful internal and external forces, the following
may not seem to be 'real'. It is an observation.

There is an idealism and inexperience with youth
which may lead to slightly wrong ideas about one's
own personal capacity to cope with temptation and its
problems. It's due to zeal and enthusiasms which young
men and women have in abundance and which they
bring to their spiritual lives. They also have a physical
strength which their elders no longer enjoy. These
natural gifts are then applied to overcome spiritual
problems. It is the way things are. But the full force of
sin and its devastating and destructive power may not
be fully appreciated in the first flush of youth – not,
that is, until there has been greater exposure to the
corruption that is in the world through lust. This comes
through the experiences of life and usually by getting
older, but not always. Sadly, some of these adverse
events come in the early years. But with inexperience it
is thought to be an easy job to 'knock over' temptations
when they arise. We need to try harder and be more
determined, we are told, and the temptation is defeated.
All you need, it is said, is more resolve, will power and
strength and the job is done.

But overcoming temptation doesn't work like that.
This attitude may lead to impatience with human
failings. This idealism will inevitably change to reality
and empathy with practical difficulties as the years roll
by and as youth matures into age.

It is not uncommon to come across a point of view
which defines some human behaviour and weaknesses
as either black or white, meaning that 'the case' is
either wrong or right. It assumes there is no grey
area, no middle way, no extenuating circumstances,

no room for regret, repentance and saying sorry. This view may imply that the conduct of the one holding this challenging opinion does not have any stain on the garment of faith and righteousness. This can hardly be, given our propensities. The only one who lived a life of right and therefore white, was the Lord Jesus, and even he on one occasion said, "Why callest thou me good? there is none good but one, that is, God".

Human beings do not come out of exactly the same mould, apart from the overall condition of mortality, with susceptibility to personal weaknesses and the impulse to sin. Character and personality are forged in the hard school of life's experiences and are a mixture of spiritual and social upbringing and living and working in an inhospitable world. No two human beings are the same; our perspectives vary because we are all in different places, physically, psychologically and spiritually. It is also a matter of knowing ourselves, our personal idiosyncrasies, our flaws, but above all being totally honest about our own individual condition, and our personal potential for weakness and temptation and therefore sin.

There is a tendency sometimes to make 'cut and dried' decisions, as if every fault or mistake is to be categorised as black and must therefore be wrong. This course of action reveals, even in the interests of justice, a 'blind spot' in the thinking and particularly in the application of spiritual principles. Although 'truth' should be paramount in both belief and behaviour – and this is the ideal – 'the truth' is not always served well when making harsh judgements in the event of personal lapses.

The Gospel of the Lord Jesus is a Gospel of reconciliation, healing and restoration. The Lord in his graciousness and mercy has seen fit to call us into his divine family. Our responsibility, if and when we have to wrestle with an individual's flaws, is to apply these same principles of reconciliation and healing, and if at all possible restore the 'offender' to the spiritual family.

We learn by practice and experience that between the extremes of black and white, there is a great gulf fixed, which is coloured grey, and that the vast majority of spiritual problems fall into this category.

This is why sometimes in ecclesial life, the 'older ones' may be perceived to be spiritually 'soft', or more liberal, or a touch too merciful. The reason is that in the latter years, the experiences of mortality are felt more keenly than in youth, and the older ones can sympathise more readily with human frailty and human problems, especially when faced with the need to make judgements in ecclesial life. The frailty is known and shared and there is a greater understanding of human nature. In this respect old age 'knows what is in man'.

When the accusers of the woman taken in adultery were invited to cast the first stone in John 8:7, Jesus prefaced his invitation with the words, "He that is without sin among you ..." It is very significant that in verse 9 they "went out one by one, beginning at the eldest, even unto the last". Why? Because they were convicted by their own conscience. The elders had a far deeper and more thorough understanding of human weakness than the younger members in the crowd and, more importantly, they had examined their own consciences and found themselves wanting. They were honest enough to recognise similar weaknesses and mistakes, the same thoughts and perhaps the same fantasies, or even the same deed. The key to all this is knowing ourselves as we are known, being absolutely honest with ourselves about failure and learning from life's experiences and situations, and what these teach us about ourselves. The corollary of this should be to apply these same principles and standards to others when they need our support.

The couplet in the Lord's Prayer, "Lead us not into temptation, but deliver us from evil", is not a throw away line, or words to be quickly passed over. They are to be considered and given full weight, for these words were offered by an understanding and compassionate Lord, as an escape route from perils and dangers which would swallow us up and destroy us when we are enticed into sin.

Breaking down our defences

In the Lord's Prayer, by the two previous petitions, the teaching is that there should be a breaking down of all those inner human defences, by which in our lack of wisdom and maturity we think we can defeat our adversaries. "Give us this day our daily bread", is the admission that we depend on God for our continuing life, and not something we can claim by right. Next, "Forgive us our debts, as we forgive our debtors", is a confession that not only can God forgive our sins, but that it is absolutely necessary that He does, if we are to have a fellowship with Him. Moreover, that reconciliation is dependent on how we relate to others, that is, "as we forgive our debtors".

So, "Lead us not into temptation, but deliver us from evil", is the final petition of the three, which confesses that our professed self-sufficiency, is in fact insufficient to defeat the tempter's onslaughts. We need to be kept in being by God, kept in His fellowship, kept away from temptation. We are not strong enough, either mentally, physically or spiritually, to engage with the forces of darkness, trial and temptation and win. Ultimately they will defeat us. We need to gather every spiritual power against them.

Peter's boastful claim

We have a striking example of 'upside down' thinking if and when we say we can defeat temptation by our own efforts, as follows:

"And the Lord said, Simon, Simon, behold, Satan hath desired to have you, that he may sift you as wheat: but I have prayed for thee, that thy faith fail not: and when thou art converted, strengthen thy brethren. And he said unto him, Lord, I am ready to go with thee, both into prison, and to death. And he

55

said, I tell thee, Peter, the cock shall not crow this day, before thou shalt thrice deny that thou knowest me." (Luke 22:31-34)

We recognise how unwisely Peter reacted against the admonition of Jesus. He boasted in his own strengths and abilities. But let's remember that Peter appears as the most proactive disciple, always out in front, testing his own faith with exploits the others would not try. In this way he built up and strengthened his faith. He learnt about the constancy of the Lord and his compassion. Of course he would go to prison, and even die for him! Who wouldn't? Peter would think to himself! Peter discovered that he fell into the temptation of denial by his own lack of caution, or his over-enthusiasm, or simply because of folly and bravado. But the challenge to his integrity, faith and love was too great. His sense of self-preservation was suddenly too overwhelming. When "he remembered the word of the Lord", his boast collapsed like his self-esteem. He had sinned and denied Christ before men. Would Christ now deny him before his Father in heaven as he had taught the disciples?

It was not the fear of death or imprisonment that defeated Peter; otherwise he wouldn't have followed Jesus to the High Priest's Palace. It was a word, a jibe, the mockery of his faith and his allegiance. It didn't come from the military, religious or the civil authorities, but from an obscure but observant servant girl. It was so unexpected and from such an unexpected source, it caught him completely off guard. He was totally unprepared for the word spoken in the firelight. He was possibly thinking of his own security, for he was in the lions' den, and perhaps considering how best he could be discreet and anonymous. He had probably forgotten his boast. He was unprepared and fell. It was not the biggest of challenges, but it demonstrates the need to be vigilant and faithful even in that which is least, and on our guard continually.

For ourselves, the further away we are from faith-compromising situations, the better. It requires a great deal of self-discipline to do this. To walk away from what could be 'harmless' fun and pleasurable activities takes courage, especially when we are encouraged to join in. What is comforting is that whilst Peter had professed his self-sufficiency and been found wanting, he was restored to fellowship with Christ. The same can be true of ourselves, even when we don't manage to fulfil the scriptural ideals set before us, or even the spiritual standards we set for ourselves. There are no exceptions to those who can be reconciled.

Jesus' own temptations

"Ye are they which have continued with me in my temptations." (Luke 22:28)

These words offer us some answers to the problems of temptation, moreover Jesus' own temptations. They are set in the context of verse 24, which describes a sad episode of group strife as to who was the greatest, and come after a warning of betrayal and identifying that the betrayer was at the same solemn table. This was just after they had broken bread together. The unity of the table was shattered by their serpent-like behaviour. At the very moment when the Lord had revealed the greatest crisis of his life, his crucifixion, they argued about their own importance and put the Lord's sufferings on hold. How the disciples' behaviour must have jarred on the mind of Jesus. He must have been agonising to bring every thought into captivity to the obedience of God, casting down imaginations, and every high thing that exalted itself against the knowledge of God (2 Corinthians 10:5). He knew what was in himself. He then gave the twelve a lesson in service and humility. They witnessed Jesus as a slave washing their feet.

Then, seemingly breaking away from his lesson, he commends them, "for ye are they which have continued with me in my temptations". Jesus is saying that the companionship of the twelve had been a great support and comfort to him during the ministry. Whilst it was true there had been fallings out and squabbles, strife even, overall they had journeyed with him. Yet they had not always understood him or his words. But they had listened to him, helped him, gone out with him and for him and engaged in the work. Three had shared the experiences of fellowship on the Mount of Transfiguration. They tried to protect him from overmuch publicity, as they thought best. They made their confession of faith in him as the Christ, the Son of the Living God, and had believed him. All this must have been a source of comfort. Now Jesus commends them. It was enough; their companionship, fellowship and support for three-and-a-half years had to some extent helped Jesus come to this point.

The same is true in our ecclesial life and wider brotherhood. The support for ecclesial projects and activities is our means of encouraging our fellows to continue in the way of life, when otherwise they might feel overwhelmed by their troubles or lost in their temptations. By and large we never know when others are walking through the valley of the shadow of death, but to be a journeying companion in faith is a source of comfort. Empty places at ecclesial meetings are a source of disappointment for those who are present, and absenteeism can be faith sapping. Our presence indicates our fellowship in Christ, our care for each other, our commitment to the cause of unity and that our association together is something we value above all else.

The disciples' temptations

Jesus refers to temptation again on the same night; twice in Luke's Gospel and both relate to the disciples' temptations:

"And he came out, and went, as he was wont, to the Mount of Olives; and his disciples also followed him. And when he was at the place, he said unto them, Pray that ye enter not into temptation ... And when he rose up from prayer, and was come to his disciples, he found them sleeping for sorrow, and he said unto them, Why sleep ye? rise and pray, lest ye enter into temptation." (22:39,40,45,46)

The evening was far spent. Tiredness and sorrow had overtaken them, but Jesus was not referring to their physical exhaustion. His thoughts had moved on to the events later that same night, to his arrest and trials, and how the eleven, with Judas Iscariot having gone from them, would react both in his defence and for their own safety. He foresaw Peter's use of the sword, his following after and denial in the High Priest's palace, and that all the others would forsake him and flee. He would be left alone without the comfort of his beloved companions, even those who, despite squabbling, had been commended for continuing with him in his temptations. Nevertheless he counsels them to "pray", and so prayer must be one of Jesus' teaching points to help combat temptation. He had himself engaged deeply in prayer and said the same words three times to reconcile his wavering thoughts with what he knew and understood perfectly as the mind of his Father. At this stage he knew his spirit was willing, even though his flesh was weak.

We are given a great lesson by Jesus in Luke 22:42 about his own attitude to temptation and testing. Knowing what he did about himself, what was required of him, who he was, and how he alone could bring about the redemption of the world, he doesn't beseech God to 'lead him not into temptation', as he had taught his disciples to pray. Instead:

"Father, if thou be willing, remove this cup from me: nevertheless not my will, but thine, be done." (verse 42)

These words are a mark of his humility and identification with us, as well as speaking of his total dependency on the greater wisdom of his Father. In the end it was his own personal decision to follow the will of his Father, as he overcame his natural inclinations to do differently. His will was brought into captivity, so that the Father's would be dominant. It was quite the opposite of Peter's bold claim.

The serpent mind

Jesus was very much aware of the mind of the serpent, and the subtlety of its arguments and its persuasiveness. He knew it could lodge within him. It's not surprising then, how frequently Jesus makes references to the serpent story of Genesis 3 in his teaching, either directly by using the same language, or indirectly by picking up the nuances and thrust of the account. Here is a case in point:

> "For where your treasure is, there will your heart be also. The light of the body is the eye: if therefore thine eye be single, thy whole body shall be full of light. But if thine eye be evil, thy whole body shall be full of darkness. If therefore the light that is in thee be darkness, how great is that darkness!"
>
> (Matthew 6:21-23)

On the face of it, it may be difficult to see a connection with the serpent and Genesis 3. But Jesus alludes to the character of the serpent with its evil eye and body full of darkness. The serpent would more than likely have been aware or even possibly overheard the conversations in the Garden of Eden between the angel and Adam and Eve, about the prohibition concerning the tree of the knowledge of good and evil and the commandment not to eat of it, but had no concept of its truth and the authority of God. It was amoral and indifferent to Adam and Eve's responsibilities. When we think about the Eve–serpent confrontation, and the simplicity with which the serpent beguiled Eve, we can see the deceptiveness of his conversation. It was only then Eve began to consider other alternatives for expressing herself and her individuality, rather than accepting the role she had been given in the Garden with its dwelling place for God and divine fellowship.

There was a time when Adam and Eve's eyes were single, when they lived in the light of the angels' presence, and when their treasure was the riches God had provided in the garden and the gift of life. But then the serpent got to work and corrupted their simplicity. It tempted them to look for an alternative way of expressing themselves, to seek equality with God and to know good and evil. Consequently their eyes became evil, and they were filled with darkness. They turned away from the light, for their hearts looked to other things for satisfaction:

"No man can serve two masters: for either he will hate the one, and love the other; or else he will hold to the one, and despise the other. Ye cannot serve God and mammon."
(verse 24)

Adam and Eve made a choice to transfer their allegiance from God to the serpent and from one master to another. They lost their love of the one, and became slaves of the other. They held on to the one, but despised the other. They probably didn't intend to despise the goodness of God, but that is what they did. They learnt by bitter experience they couldn't serve both God and mammon. The clash of the demands of the two masters meant they pleased neither. They lost the fellowship of God but could not escape the authority and servitude imposed by the serpent. In a sense they became aimless with no loyalties.

"Therefore I say unto you, Take no thought for your life, what ye shall eat, or what ye shall drink; nor yet for your body, what ye shall put on. Is not the life more than meat, and the body than raiment?"
(verse 25)

The serpent persuaded Adam and Eve to be discontented with the life God had given them, which was for living to His glory. But after their graceless act of disobedience they did take thought for their lives, and what they should eat and drink. They even thought about what clothes they should wear. Before the fall, "they were both naked ... and were not ashamed". Unfortunately, because they were beguiled into wrong thinking, their food and drink and aspirations were seen to be of more value than life itself. They failed to hold on to the purpose for which God had given them life and dominion over His creation. "Which of you by taking thought can add one cubit unto his stature?" (verse 27).

The serpent told Adam and Eve they could add to their "stature" – not their physical height but their estimation of themselves, their own perceived standing and importance among the angels, and presumably over the animals of the creation. To be as gods knowing good and evil, and seeking equality with God was exaltation and a prize to be grasped. That was adding to their stature – it puffed them up. "Knowledge puffeth up" says the Apostle Paul. But Adam and Eve soon found that puffed up pride is easily deflated.

"Take therefore no thought for the morrow: for the morrow shall take thought for the things of itself. Sufficient unto the day is the evil thereof." (verse 34) This is a hard lesson to learn, and unfortunately Adam and Eve did not until they were ejected from the Garden. It meant they were discontented with the situation God had provided, as well as the place and role He had given them for their good and spiritual development. They had forgotten, or chose to harbour doubts, that God could provide for tomorrow, and thought they needed to make their own plans. They did not learn until too late that each day will bring its share of evil and trouble, and the testing of faith, and temptations which need to be challenged. They were unable – and we find it equally difficult – to live each day as the gift of God, and take no thought about tomorrow.

The knowledge of God

In Matthew 6, Jesus teaches us to have an awareness of the knowledge and power of God. Although "unseen, He is ever near"; further, our "angels behold the face of [our] Father which is in heaven" (Matthew 18:10). The following three passages from Matthew 6 qualify three different aspects of Christian endeavour: our giving, praying and personal discipline. Although they do not appear to be directly related to temptation, the wisdom recorded can prevent us falling by subtle ways into temptation.

"... that thine alms may be in secret: and thy Father which seeth in secret himself shall reward thee openly ... But thou, when thou prayest, enter into thy closet, and when thou hast shut thy door, pray to thy Father which is in secret; and thy Father which seeth in secret shall reward thee openly ... that thou appear not unto men to fast, but unto thy Father which is in secret: and thy Father, which seeth in secret, shall reward thee openly."

(Matthew 6:4,6,18)

How can these three verses help us? We could be tempted to broadcast the extent of our giving, by making comparisons with others and their apparent meanness; or be tempted to make our prayers a show of the finest language to the exclusion of real content; or be tempted to proclaim the piety of our Christian life, and that we are close and determined followers of Christ. We don't have to do or say anything publicly; it could all be in the mind. Jesus has one word for all this – hypocrisy – and reminds us that the Father which sees in secret shall reward us openly.

This teaching seems to be a distillation of the first part of Psalm 139:

"O LORD, thou hast searched me, and known me. Thou knowest my downsitting and mine uprising, thou understandest my thought afar off. Thou compassest my path and my lying down, and art acquainted with all my ways. For there is not a word in my tongue, but, lo, O LORD, thou knowest it altogether."   (verses 1-4)

If only we could convert this declaration of the omniscience of God into a living reality, so we constantly live in His presence and know that we do. If only we could do this twenty-four hours a day and seven days a week, how much more positive would our lives be; to remember that God is watching every action, listening to every conversation, marking every place we visit, noting all we watch and read and who we socialise with. But that's exactly how it is. He does know, watch, mark and note. The trouble is, we don't always remember to live like this 'twenty-four seven', because we forget; or we are drawn away by our own lusts and our deceitful hearts, which seize us by our heels and beguile us.

We have considered briefly some of the guidance Jesus has given to help us deal with our own temptations. He has told us the answer is found in our prayers, our spiritual foundations, our fellowship of support, and our awareness of the omniscience and omnipresence of God. But he has also made us aware of the subtleties of the mind of the serpent.

6

INTO THE WILDERNESS

"Then was Jesus led up of the Spirit into the wilderness."

SO opens the temptation narrative in Matthew Chapter 4. Being "led up of the Spirit" may convey an unwillingness to go, but Mark's Gospel in 1:12 tells us, "And immediately the Spirit driveth him into the wilderness", which implies a reluctance to go. Mark's account may be expressing the thoughts and feelings of Jesus.

The word Mark uses for "driveth" is *ekballo*. Strong's Concordance indicates that its meaning includes, 'to eject, cast forth, cast out, drive out, expel, thrust out, put forth, send away'. We can appreciate there is a force being applied in order to accomplish the task. The Greek word *ekballo* is a compound of two other words – *ek* meaning 'from, out of' (as in *ecclesia*) and *ballo*, meaning 'to throw (in various applications more or less violent or intense), send, thrust'. This word *ballo* in turn is a part of *diaballo*, 'to traduce, accuse'; and also of *diabolos,* 'the false accuser, devil, slanderer'. These uses make it clear that *ballo* is another very forceful word with strong action. In the circumstances we can understand why Mark 1:12 uses the word "driveth", implying perhaps some reluctance on the part of Jesus knowing what was to befall him at the end of the journey.

It would be most unusual, given that Jesus was born of flesh and blood and tempted in all points like as we are, for him not to respond initially in this way and hesitate. But much more, Jesus had vowed to honour the will of his Father. He knew the scripture:

"Lo, I come: in the volume of the book it is written of me, I delight to do thy will, O my God: yea, thy law is within my heart." (Psalm 40:7,8)

Whatever occurred at this crucial moment in time, Jesus was "led" or "driven" into the wilderness for testing.

The temptation narrative in Luke 4:1, after the baptism record and the Mary genealogy, begins, "Jesus being full of the Holy Spirit returned from Jordan, and was led by the Spirit into the wilderness". This means that the wilderness of the temptations was not the same place as the valley of the River Jordan where Jesus was baptized by John the Baptist. The question then arises, in which wilderness did the temptations take place? We cannot be certain, but it is likely to be in the south of the country in the Judaean Hills, or in the Wilderness of Zin, or the Negev, or even the Wilderness of Paran, the same territory where the Children of Israel had their testing. If this were the case it would be most appropriate. The book of Deuteronomy and the prophet Jeremiah some nine hundred years later, both describe this desert as very unfriendly and inhospitable:

"... who led thee through that great and terrible wilderness, wherein were fiery serpents, and scorpions, and drought, where there was no water; who brought thee forth water out of the rock of flint; who fed thee in the wilderness with manna, which thy fathers knew not, that he might humble thee, and that he might prove thee, to do thee good at thy latter end." (Deuteronomy 8:15,16)

"He found him in a desert land, and in the waste howling wilderness; he led him about, he instructed him, he kept him as the apple of his eye." (32:10)

"The LORD ... that led us through the wilderness, through a land of deserts and of pits, through a land of drought, and of the shadow of death, through a land that no man passed through, and where no man dwelt." (Jeremiah 2:6)

This picture of a barren, lonely, waterless landscape, with a cloud of death hanging over it, emphasises a desperate fear that could grip any who found themselves there. It would take a strong man to overcome and survive in this extreme environment. Allowing for this description of the "great and terrible wilderness", perhaps we begin to understand why the Children of Israel complained to Moses. This is not to excuse their rebellion, as Moses called their complaining, but just to highlight their hardships given the family make-up of the congregation, and the anxieties some would have about the less able and the young. This could then have been the same place where Jesus experienced his trials and testing for forty days and nights. The purpose was the same in each case, "to humble thee, and to prove thee, to know what was in thine heart ... to do thee good at thy latter end". When we read Mark's account again with its added information, "and was with the wild beasts", it is similar to this passage in Deuteronomy 8.

Temptation from within

I am of the view that the three wilderness temptations and all the others experienced sprang from the heart and mind of Jesus. It is acknowledged that there are different views about this. Some hold there was an external tempter present in the wilderness with Jesus, being responsible for and taking part in the temptations.[1] It has been suggested that it was an angel from heaven,[2] or perhaps a human adversary or agency, such as the Jewish High Priest, or possibly the Roman governor or even the Roman Emperor. Orthodoxy of course, teaches that this tempter was no less than the supernatural personal being, known as the devil, or the *diabolos*.

It is worth noting how one such argument has been presented to support the supernatural tempter. In acknowledging that the temptation narrative is a history of an actual occurrence, it is asserted in the

---

1 Brother Robert Roberts, *Nazareth Revisited,* 2nd edition, 1916, page 85.
2 Brother John Thomas, *Eureka,* Volume 3, 1918 edition, page 65.

following paragraph that the temptation was by the devil as a person:

"This interpretation ... presupposes two things, which are also supposed throughout the rest of scripture: the possibility of the supernatural, and the personality of the Tempter. If either of these is denied, the fundamental doctrines of the Christian Faith must necessarily fall with them. To deny the supernatural is to deny what is asserted in every page of the Gospels; and to deny the personality of the Tempter is virtually to assert that the temptation was suggested from within, not from without – an assertion incompatible with the perfect sinlessness of Christ, and with all the edifice of Christian truth, of which that sinlessness is the foundation. The naturalistic explanations, such as that which supposes the tempter to have been a man, or the whole scene to have taken place in a dream or a trance, are contrary to the whole tenor of the narrative."[3]

This piece from the *Speaker's Commentary* strongly supports the notion that the tempter was the literal devil and therefore external. On the basis of the false doctrine that the devil is supernatural and has an independent personality, incorrect conclusions have been drawn about the nature of Christ and his temptations. This view has been propped up by another false idea, that Jesus Christ is God the Son, the second part of the Trinity and of divine nature, embodied in a man. We must not make the mistake of holding views which are supported only by wrong doctrine. As was explained earlier, Jesus shared our own flawed nature with all its propensities for sin and wrongdoing, and was himself subject to death because of that hereditary factor. Consequently, the argument presented in the *Speaker's Commentary* collapses when set alongside the true Biblical teaching. Others will no doubt agree or disagree

3 *Speaker's Commentary* on Matthew's Gospel, published 1878, New Testament, Volume 1, page 17.

with these conclusions and make up their own minds on the basis of the evidence as they read and interpret it.[4]

So for the reasons advanced I believe there was no external tempter. He was on his own in the wilderness: he needed to be. The force of the temptation came from within him, as it comes from within every man and woman, as emphasised in James 1:14,15 and Hebrews 2:14,18. We may not like to think this about Jesus, and would prefer it was different. But when we understand that he had the same nature as ourselves, and was capable of the same kinds of thoughts, and could have had exactly the same kinds of responses, we marvel that he overcame the temptations at all.

The Gospels say that Jesus was accompanied only by "wild beasts", and at the end of the forty-day period was sustained by the angels. This use of the plural tells us there was more than one. How many we cannot say. By contrast, when in the Garden of Gethsemane and the final trial was upon him, his prayers to his Father for an alternative way other than the cross, were answered by "an angel". The inference is only one angel. But that is not to say the Gethsemane examination was any less agonising or painful than the wilderness experience when there were at least two. One angel was sufficient to provide the necessary comfort and support. The two or more angels at the end of the forty days and nights, as well as supplying his needs, could also have been encouraging Jesus and rejoicing in the triumphant victory just accomplished – the Father's way of saying again, "In whom I am well pleased". This was the first major crisis of his life when flesh and spirit would clash. One wonders if the angels included "the angel of [God's] presence", who was appointed to supervise the welfare of the Children of Israel, and Gabriel who apprised

4 Brother H. A. Whittaker, *Studies in the Gospels*, 1st edition, 1985, pages 67-69, has a most useful eight-point analysis of the problems involved if another person or being, whether human or divine, were present with Jesus in the wilderness during the temptations.

Mary of his conception and birth. We cannot be sure, but it would be quite fitting.

Forty days and nights

"And when he had fasted forty days and forty nights, he was afterward an hungered."

(Matthew 4:2)

When would hunger pains first arise? Naturally he would be hungry at the end of the first day and certainly by the second or third day. But the spirit had set a time period of forty days and nights during which a fast was to be observed. Afterwards he hungered. Forty days and nights are clearly meant to recall the forty-year period of the Children of Israel in their wilderness journey. Both Jesus and the Children of Israel were firstborn sons of God; both had been called out of Egypt; both were sons of the spirit and of promise. The nation was born by the reawakening of Abraham and Sarah, and Jesus was born when the Holy Spirit came upon Mary.

But questions have been asked about the Lord's ability to sustain himself without food or water for forty days and nights, in a waste howling great and terrible wilderness. Did he have a miraculous supply of water, and did he pick food from off such trees as he could find?

There are scriptural precedents for forty days and nights. Elijah and Moses, who were to join Jesus on the Mount of Transfiguration later in the ministry, both experienced forty days and nights in same wilderness and on the same mountain. It's instructive to look at the situations surrounding them. First, Elijah:

"And he arose, and did eat and drink, and went in the strength of that meat forty days and forty nights unto Horeb the mount of God."   (1 Kings 19:8)

Elijah had been in Mount Carmel with four hundred prophets of Baal and had fled to Beersheba on learning of Jezebel's threat on his life. His angelic experience (verses 5-7) provided his food and drink, and this was to sustain him for the next six weeks as he journeyed to Horeb. He ate "angels' food" (Psalm 78:25). At Horeb in the cleft of the rock he had the frightening experience of the tempest, the earthquake and the fire, before he heard "a still small voice", the word of God. Listening to this provided his strength and resolve to face the rigours of the wilderness and his ministry, and defeat the diabolical Jezebel together with her paganism.

Now the record about Moses:

"And Moses went into the midst of the cloud, and gat him up into the mount: and Moses was in the mount forty days and forty nights." (Exodus 24:18)

This is the account of Moses receiving the law for the first time when in the presence of the angel of the Lord for forty days and nights, during his sojourn on the top of Mount Sinai. We note how the top of the mount (verse 17) appeared to be on fire with the glory of the Lord. Just after the great theophany of the name of the Lord, when he was pressed into a cleft on the rock face, Moses had his second opportunity to receive the law from the angel:

"And the LORD said unto Moses, Write thou these words: for after the tenor of these words I have made a covenant with thee and with Israel. And he was there with the LORD forty days and forty nights; he did neither eat bread, nor drink water. And he wrote upon the tables the words of the covenant, the ten commandments. And it came to pass, when Moses came down from mount Sinai with the two tables of testimony in Moses' hand, when he came down from the mount, that Moses wist not that the skin of his face shone while he talked with him. And when Aaron and all the children of Israel saw Moses, behold, the skin of his face shone; and they were afraid to come nigh him." (Exodus 34:27-30)

Another forty days and nights in Horeb without bread and water, yet he had sufficient strength at the end of his vigil to carry down the mountain two heavy tables of stone written with ten commandments. Moses repeats these descriptions in Deuteronomy 9:9,11,18,25, emphasising forty days and forty nights without bread and water.

These occasions in the lives of Elijah and Moses demonstrate that it is possible to survive forty days and nights in a wilderness situation without food and water. Jesus would know the patterns, the place, and the outcome, and that both Elijah and Moses had heard the "still small voice" and were obedient to it. We have no indication of the physical toll which was taken on either Moses or Elijah, but we do have the recorded facts that Moses carried two heavy stones down the mountain which is said to be 2,244 metres high (or 7,362 feet above sea level – a quarter of the height of Mount Everest) and that Elijah was able to withstand the forces of the weather, albeit secured by the protection of the rock face. So it is possible both to endure and survive forty days and nights of fasting, whilst engaging in other strenuous activities whether physical, mental or spiritual. At least they did in Bible times!

Christ's baptism

Before we look at the first temptation of turning stones into bread, we shall briefly consider the baptism narrative again:

"Then cometh Jesus from Galilee to Jordan unto John, to be baptized of him. But John forbad him, saying, I have need to be baptized of thee, and comest thou to me? And Jesus answering said unto him, Suffer it to be so now: for thus it becometh us to fulfil all righteousness. Then he suffered him. And Jesus, when he was baptized, went up straightway out of the water: and, lo, the heavens were opened unto him, and he saw the spirit of God descending like a dove, and lighting upon him." (Matthew 3:13-16)

Jesus' submission to the water baptism of John the Baptist was on the basis that "it becometh us to fulfil all righteousness". Human nature deserved only death by virtue of the mortality which came as a result of the disobedience of Adam and Eve, and their legacy fell on all their descendants. Jesus was included in this, as both the Matthew and Luke genealogies show. When Jesus came up out of the water there was "a voice from heaven, saying, This is my beloved Son, in whom I am well pleased" (verse 17). This declaration is a combination of words taken from Psalm 2 and Isaiah 42: "Thou art my Son; this day have I begotten thee" (Psalm 2:7) and, "Behold my servant, whom I uphold; mine elect, in whom my soul delighteth; I have put my spirit upon him: he shall bring forth judgment to the Gentiles" (Isaiah 42:1).

In the Psalm 2 passage, and in fulfilling the promises to David, Messiah is presented as occupying the throne. It refers to his resurrection glory, and the eventual completion of the purpose of redemption. The second half of verse 7 was spoken from heaven at the baptism of Jesus, and then the voice included part of Isaiah 42:1. The Isaiah passage tells of the ideal servant who is both co-operative and obedient, and who would constantly do the will of God: therefore, "in whom I am well pleased", or "in whom my soul delighteth".

The Greek here may not just mean, "with whom I am delighted", but perhaps additionally 'in whom my pleasure rests', or 'of whom I have thought well'. One commentator[5] has suggested that it's possible to include 'in whom my plan of salvation for mankind is centred', picking up the idea of the fulfilment of God's ultimate pleasure, which was one of the objectives of his baptism.

The voice which came from heaven declared Jesus to be (1) God's beloved Son, and (2) the servant on whom God would rely to bring about the promised salvation; and what is more, this depended on the perfect co-operation and obedience of that servant. Consequently, if Jesus had placed too much emphasis on the first part of the message from heaven, "Thou art my Son", there could have been the temptation to take the glory of the kingdom in the days of his flesh, at the expense of second part, when he was declared to be the faithful, obedient servant, "in whom my pleasure rests", and in whom the purpose of salvation depended for unfolding and completion.

5 *Tyndale New Testament Commentaries, Matthew*, Professor R. V. G. Tasker, 1963 reprint, page 51, additional note 17.

Jesus' purpose as both the Son and the Servant was to be willingly submissive to the overriding authority of God, and not decide for himself when and how he would satisfy his desires. Obedience was his watchword, and his Father was the provider of every good and perfect gift. As the first temptation came to him, he needed to resolve in his own heart that as he had been driven into the wilderness, and had been subjected to forty days and nights of hunger and fasting, and had been preserved thus far, his Father would provide him with whatever was needful – but in the Father's own good time.

7

COMMAND THAT THESE STONES BE MADE BREAD

THE temptation to make stones into bread is not concerned with casting any doubt on Jesus' Sonship, although that could be implied from the subtle statement made by the tempter; but rather with providing a way for him to avoid the servant role, and getting him to deny the perfect obedience expected of the servant, who was also to be a true son of God. The temptation is about the lust of flesh, and was a challenge to Jesus' dependency on God to supply all his needs. His loyalty and obedience to God were under attack.

"And when the tempter came to him, he said, If thou be the Son of God, command that these stones be made bread." (Matthew 4:3)

"If thou be the Son of God": this was not expressing a doubt – there was *no* doubt. He had heard the voice from heaven declare that plainly. But now an inner voice was saying, 'Because you are the Son of God, what powers you have! Prove you are the Son of God to your people, but first satisfy your own essential and personal needs!' The privilege and responsibility of being the Son of God lay heavily on him. How would he respond and show his love to his Father?

"Command that these stones be made bread"! This 'command' did not thunder out across the barren empty landscape. It was the awakened inner voice of the flesh thinking about all the possibilities and the wants and needs of the flesh. It was whispered internally, and invitingly. Bread represents everything natural and essential to life. God provides bread as a gift to satisfy a God-created need, our hunger. It is not sinful to satisfy such a need. Perhaps the bread baked in first century ovens looked like stones. Or was Jesus thinking of the manna in the wilderness experience of the children of Israel? The answer came swiftly:

"It is written, Man shall not live by bread alone, but by every word that proceedeth out of the mouth of God."   (4:4)

This firm response is taken from Deuteronomy 8:3, although Matthew and Luke record only the relevant part of this Old Testament passage. It does not mean that daily bread is unnecessary, for clearly it is. But for a balanced, healthy, spiritual, beneficial life, and a life which will honour God by doing His commandments, the word of God is needed as well. What is the power and value of this word? How does it help man to 'live' eternally – live by every word which proceeds out of the mouth of the Lord? To discover the answer to these questions, we need to consider the accounts of the Children of Israel as they journeyed in their wilderness.

The proving of the Children of Israel

"All the commandments which I command thee this day shall ye observe to do, that ye may live, and multiply, and go in and possess the land which the LORD sware unto your fathers. And thou shalt remember all the way which the LORD thy God led thee these forty years in the wilderness, to humble thee, and to prove thee, to know what was in thine heart, whether thou wouldest keep his commandments, or no. And he humbled thee, and suffered thee to hunger, and fed thee with manna, which thou knewest not, neither did thy fathers know; that he might make thee know that man doth not live by bread only, but by every word that proceedeth out of the mouth of the LORD, doth man live. Thy raiment waxed not old upon thee, neither did thy foot swell, these forty years. Thou shalt also consider in thine heart, that, as a man chasteneth his son, so the LORD thy God chasteneth thee. Therefore thou shalt keep the commandments of the LORD thy God, to walk in his ways, and to fear him."   (Deuteronomy 8:1-6)

After their settlement in the promised land, the Israelites would be in danger from the temptation of falling into pride and forgetfulness of God, when enjoying the abundant produce and wealth of the land. To guard against this danger, Moses set out how God had hoped to bring them to obedience by their testing and afflictions during the wilderness journey. The ultimate objective for them (8:1) was that they should live and multiply and attain to the full possession of the promised land. To this end they were to remember (verse 2) the forty years of guidance by the Angel of His Presence (Exodus 23:20; 33:14) by which God desired to humble them, and to test the state of their hearts and obedience to His commandments. Humbling them was the way God had chosen so that the people could prove to themselves their attitude towards Him, and be brought by means of distresses and privations to feel in need of His help and know their total dependence on the Covenant God. He would prove them by placing them in situations which would cause them to reveal their true selves, expose what was really in their hearts and whether they believed in the omnipotence, love, and righteousness of God or not.

The opening phrase of Deuteronomy 8:3 in the Septuagint (LXX) is very powerful: "And he afflicted thee and straitened thee with hunger". The word "straitened" (Greek, *agcheo*) is the root word for 'strangled or throttled', and we can almost feel the force and strength of the idea presented. *Agcheo* occurs only this once in the Greek Old Testament text. The suffering described was, and should have been, a national humbling experience. Not only did God let the people hunger, but He also fed them with manna. This daily provision was part of the humbling process, because it showed that they did not live only by their oven baked home-made bread, or that the power to sustain life resides only in the bread, but that life – real life, the fullness of life – depends upon what goes out of the mouth of the Lord; that is, true life depends on what God says and supplies.

77

That which "proceedeth out of the mouth of the LORD", is not just the word of the law, but the revealed will of God and His promise to preserve the life of men and women by whatever means He chooses. It is with this emphasis that Jesus refers to these words from Deuteronomy in his reply to the tempter. He did *not* say, 'I do not live only by physical bread, or by the fulfilment of the will of God, or by trusting in the word of God'; but *rather*, 'I leave it to God to care for my daily life as only He can, as He knows best and will do it, in extraordinary ways with extraordinary supplies, and by the power of His almighty word and will'.

It was in this way that God humbled and tested His people, that they should learn in their hearts (verses 5,6) and become convinced in themselves that their God was educating them as a father does his son, with admonishments and chastening but most of all with love. The purpose of their education was to train them to keep His commandments, that they should walk in His ways and fear Him; but above all, to love Him with all their heart, soul, mind and strength. All this was part of the Lord Jesus' meditation during the forty days of his trial. He knew that keeping, trusting and believing the word from heaven was the key to the life of the Eternal, and the inheritance of things to come.

When Moses said (verse 2), "to humble thee, and to prove thee, to know what was in thine heart, whether thou wouldest keep his commandments, or no", he was referring to the days when God first provided the manna forty years earlier.

God provides manna

In Exodus 16 there are complaints about hunger, and the desire for Egypt and its fleshpots with the fullness of bread; but more seriously there is the people's unbelief about God's promised redemption. These events occurred just four weeks or thirty days out of Egypt, and the whole congregation murmured!

"Then said the LORD unto Moses, Behold, I will rain bread from heaven for you; and the people shall go out and gather a certain rate every day, that I may prove them, whether they will walk in my law, or no."

(Exodus 16:4)

Gathering manna on a daily basis was a test of their faith in the word, that when God said He would supply it, He would! But they needed to go out and collect it. They had to believe God's word that the manna would be there six mornings each week and that He was as good as His word, especially as their food stocks were virtually non-existent and their pantries empty. This would be especially important the morning before the sabbath. "Whether they will walk in my law, or no": this phrase will repeat as "keep his commandments, or no" in Deuteronomy 8:2. The people were rebellious and ungrateful for the daily miracle, and their actions revealed their unbelief:

"Notwithstanding they hearkened not unto Moses; but some of them left of it until the morning, and it bred worms, and stank: and Moses was wroth with them." (Exodus 16:20)

"They hearkened not", led to their pride and obstinacy, the very opposite of the humility required by Deuteronomy 8:2,3. This was the purpose for which "he afflicted thee and straitened thee with hunger". They were led into proud ways because they chose not to listen, and promoted themselves at the expense of God and the instruction of His servant Moses. This was tantamount to not being humbled by the wonder of the daily miraculous provision of manna, coupled with behaviour that offended God. Moses was God's spokesman: to ignore Moses was to ignore God; to ignore God was rebellion – that was sinful.

Moses had said, 'Don't leave any of it until the morning'. But they did! And it stank! The people's greed, or caution, or doubts, or rank disobedience, worked against them, and brought Moses' judgements down on them. Moses had said, 'God has provided for us today, and He will again tomorrow'. But the people wouldn't or couldn't believe this. This was not living by every word

79

of God, or even believing that God was true to His word. It was rejecting that God was capable of doing what He said, or that He had the power to fulfil His promises. Flexing the muscles of the flesh is rebellion and sinful.

"Consider in thine heart"

Jesus' own testing and proving was patterned on the instructions of God to the nation. It was concerned with relationships and fellowship. In the case of Israel, rebuilding and reconnecting a broken relationship; and in the case of Jesus, strengthening an already strong fellowship with the Father. Jesus was tested as he prepared for his new service. He needed to know what was really lodging deep within his own heart: "that the things in thine heart might be made manifest, whether thou wouldest keep his commandments or no" (Deuteronomy 8:2, LXX).

Jesus "knew what was in man", because he was a man himself and it was 'in him'. He knew the heart as the origin of rebellion. So the heart had to be changed. The 'diabolical' tendencies that rose up unbidden from within must be conquered every time and for all time. The only sure way was testing and more testing, and for him to be repeatedly reminded of what he needed to do, until his unfailing obedience was second nature. His love would be fully revealed.

"Thou shall also consider in thine heart, that, as a man chasteneth his son, so the LORD thy God chasteneth thee." (8:5)

The phrase, "as a man chasteneth his son" is alluded to later in the Old Testament, particularly in the Proverbs and is applied in the first place to the Solomon-Rehoboam relationship. But the underlying family relationship that is described is that of the Father in heaven and Jesus His Spirit-born Son of promise.

"My son, despise not the chastening of the LORD; neither be weary of his correction: for whom the LORD loveth he correcteth; even as a father the son in whom he delighteth." (Proverbs 3:11,12)

For Jesus this would be helpful because he was the Son. But the chastening of the Lord could be irksome, perhaps even frustrating. Maybe it would be painful when the flesh was awakened. But Jesus would know that he was loved because of this inner conflict, and that his Father 'delighted' in him. The Father had said so at his baptism, reminding him of the faithful promise of Isaiah 42:1, for a servant who remained loyal.

All of the Father's chastening created the obedient Son. He had endured forty days and nights of hardship. He learned his obedience by the things which he suffered. He knew by learning and now by experience that natural things like bread are only temporal, but spiritual things are eternal. It was a matter of waiting on the providence of God, denying the lust of wanting and avoiding the frustration caused by being unsatisfied, because he couldn't have them when he wanted them. It was a lesson in patience and longsuffering, waiting for the Omnipotent God who is outside time to work in the life of one who is bound by time; and then to believe that the answer whenever or however it came was *right*, to the eternal good of the believer, whatever the temporal hardship.

What did the Deuteronomy passage mean to Jesus? He would learn that he must be full of faith, for his own life had been described by Moses. The children of Israel were actually re-living his life, and not doing it very well, rather than Jesus having to pattern his life on that of the early nation.

Moses had said, "Thou shalt remember all the way" (Deuteronomy 8:2). That was the key. 'Do not forget the promises sworn with an oath to the fathers of old.' And what promises! Here was everything that was the foundation stone of the nation; the very reason why it had to come into being. It was at the same time both the natural and the spiritual basis of the nation. The promises and the oath were two immutable things which could not be broken. It was God's way, His will and His word that was best. What is wonderful, is that this learning was translated into daily living by the

Master, and then into precepts for all his disciples, including those who would come after and walk in the same way. By this kind of single-minded faith, even if there is not the same degree of 'success', disciples can be partakers of the promised life.

In the power of the Spirit

According to Exodus 34:29-35, when Moses came down from Horeb the second time carrying the two heavy tables of stone, after spending a second forty days and nights in the presence of God, he "wist not that the skin of his face shone". Consequently the children of Israel could not look on Moses' face, and he was asked to put a veil over it until the glory faded.

This event is expounded in 2 Corinthians 3:13-16, where the veiling of Moses' face is likened to the veil spread over the hearts of the Children of Israel who failed to see the Sonship and the glory of Christ. Their hearts were hard, like the two tables of stone. But consider these words from earlier in the same chapter:

"Ye are our epistle written in our hearts, known and read of all men: forasmuch as ye are manifestly declared to be the epistle of Christ ministered by us, written not with ink, but with the Spirit of the living God; not in tables of stone, but in fleshy tables of the heart." (2 Corinthians 3:2,3)

Those who hear, receive, and believe that the word is the epistle written by God and comes from God, have it written not on tables of stone, but in "fleshy tables of the heart", unveiled hearts, open hearts inclined to God. "Fleshy" in this context is not used to denote the natural state of men or the 'lusts of the heart', but rather the soft, pliable and easily entreated hearts and minds that willingly receive the divine letters, to be written "with the Spirit of the living God". Becoming themselves the epistle of Christ, which can be read and known of all men and proclaimed by the very lives which are lived, their hearts are touched by the gentleness and power of the "still small voice". Such was the heart and mind of Jesus, as he came out of the wilderness at the end of forty days and nights, "in the power of the Spirit", proceeding to Galilee, but also steeled against the rigours of the ministry which was just beginning.

8

SET ON A PINNACLE OF THE TEMPLE

IT is possible that the prophetic teaching of Psalm 2 could have provided the basis for each of the three temptations experienced by the Lord in his lonely wilderness sojourn:

"Yet have I set my king upon my holy hill of Zion. I will declare the decree: the LORD hath said unto me, Thou art my Son; this day have I begotten thee. Ask of me, and I shall give thee the heathen for thine inheritance, and the uttermost parts of the earth for thy possession." (Psalm 2:6-8)

This is a Messianic psalm, with references to his birth, baptism, death and resurrection and ultimate kingdom glory.

Verse 6 is part of the substance of the second temptation – the holy hill of Zion and the city of the great King. He was the designated King; Zion was his promised city. We shall explore this further as we examine the detail of the "pinnacle of the temple".

Verse 7 – "Thou art my Son": this is connected to the first temptation and the Lord's ministry to satisfy the people's need, by feeding them with bread from heaven and the riches of the word of God – if only they would have received it. We have already seen how this text was referred to by the voice from heaven at Jesus' baptism.

Verse 8 – this has reference to the third temptation, as "the uttermost parts of the earth" for his inheritance refers to his kingship, his reign over all the peoples of the earth as God's appointed ruler, and the establishment of the kingdom.

The tempter

I have used the term 'the tempter' because this is a word the Gospel writer used. The usual Greek word employed in the temptation accounts is *diabolos*, as seen in the table below, and commonly translated 'devil'. In fact the Emphatic Diaglott presents the appropriate words of the Gospel records as follows:

Ref.	Greek text	English Inter-linear literal	Diaglott 'New' Version	AV/RV
Matthew 4				
v. 1	*diabolos*	accuser	enemy	devil
v. 3	*peirazo*	tempter	tempter	tempter
v. 5	*diabolos*	accuser	enemy	devil
v. 8	*diabolos*	accuser	enemy	devil
v. 10	*satanas*	adversary	adversary	satan
v. 11	*diabolos*	accuser	enemy	devil
Mark 1:13	*satanas*	adversary	adversary	satan
Luke 4				
v. 2	*diabolos*	accuser	enemy	devil
v. 3	*diabolos*	accuser	enemy	devil
v. 5	*diabolos*	accuser	he	devil/he
v. 6	*diabolos*	accuser	enemy	devil
v. 8	*satanas*	him	him	satan
v. 13	*diabolos*	accuser	enemy	devil

What is the devil, *ho diabolos*? In our public talks we stress that *ho diabolos* is the false accuser, the slanderer, the adversary, the one that strikes through. We also stress that the devil is not a literal personal superhuman devil, as is commonly believed by orthodoxy, but our very selves. It is the umbrella term for the 'sin power' which comes in many disguises, but which is always in opposition to God's righteous laws and those who believe and follow them.

As concerning ourselves and personal sin, we are quite definite that an external tempter does *not* prompt it, but that we are drawn away of our own lusts; it comes from within from our own minds and hearts. Jeremiah 17:9, James 1:14,15 and Mark 7:14-23 are just three of the references used to support this teaching, in addition to Hebrews 2:14. In considering this in connection with the temptations of Jesus we must be consistent:

> "Then the devil taketh him up into the holy city, and setteth him on a pinnacle of the temple, and saith unto him, If thou be the Son of God, cast thyself down: for it is written, He shall give his angels charge concerning thee: and in their hands they shall bear thee up, lest at any time thou dash thy foot against a stone. Jesus saith unto him, It is written again, Thou shalt not tempt the Lord thy God." (Matthew 4:5-7)

I am not going to deal with the different order in the two Gospels or why this is so. It might mean that the same temptation occurred more than once during the forty days and nights whilst Jesus was in the wilderness.

This second temptation is concerned with the "pride of life". "Cast thyself down", the tempter said. Jesus was being encouraged to be a stuntman, and do some heroics for self-aggrandisement. All this was a denial of God's way and not far removed from 'you shall be as gods, to know ...' His trust in God was under threat.

Jesus was still in the wilderness. What triggered the thoughts of pinnacles and the temple? What was Jesus thinking about in the silence and isolation of the wilderness?

What do we think about in the imaginations of our own hearts and what are our musings in the quietness of the night watches? We are all familiar with how shadows and silences and the half-light of evenings or early mornings can play tricks on our ears and eyes – when we think we've seen something or heard someone move, only to discover that it is the wind or moving clouds. Perhaps Jesus saw in the mountain peaks of his hostile environment the friendly pinnacles of the temple with which he was so familiar. Perhaps he imagined the temple. In any event, in thought Jesus went to Jerusalem and to its highest corner some 650 feet above the Kidron Valley. It would command a magnificent view east across this valley to the Mount of Olives and south over the Judaean hills. There on the highest of hills was his beloved Jerusalem.

The holy city

Luke 4:9 records, "And he [the devil] brought him to Jerusalem". It was the dwelling place of God, the city in which his Father had chosen to put His name. It was the apple of God's eye Jesus might have been thinking about. What scriptures would come to mind telling of Jerusalem and his part in its future? Amongst many, perhaps the following:

"Great is the LORD, and greatly to be praised in the city of our God, in the mountain of his holiness. Beautiful for situation, the joy of the whole earth, is mount Zion, on the sides of the north, the city of the great King. God is known in her palaces for a refuge." (Psalm 48:1-3)

Note the links with Matthew 4:5 – "the holy city", together with her designated King. God should have been known and praised there and yet He was not. It was for the Son to declare Him, to prepare the city for the coming of the great King. This was the work of the ministry to come, but there was not a positive response, for "he came unto his own, and his own received him not" (John 1:11). How he dearly would have liked to persuade the city to turn to God and convert, but he knew Isaiah 6:9,10 and the stubbornness of his people. He doubtless reflected on their rejection of him and anticipated his sadness as they turned away from him. But, "[the Gospel] shall not have gone over the cities of Israel till the Son of man be come" (Matthew 10:23).

Did he consider that it was part of his mission to press for the fulfilment of other psalms before the time was right? He would know the temple songs of Psalms 18, 45-49 and 136 for example, and how such hymns

87

had once resounded through the temple to the glory of his Father, each accompanied by orchestra and choirs in times past. He would have hoped that such could be the case again even in his earthly days, when the joy of the true worship would be offered by sincere and God-fearing people. Holiness would bind all true hearts together; the world would be healed and at peace.

As he gazed upon the peaks of the wilderness and thought about the temple pinnacles in Jerusalem, perhaps he would muse on the fulfilment of the great temple psalm of David, and Solomon's prayer at the dedication of his Father's designed and chosen dwelling-place:

"For the LORD hath chosen Zion; he hath desired it for his habitation. This is my rest for ever: here will I dwell; for I have desired it. I will abundantly bless her provision: I will satisfy her poor with bread. I will also clothe her priests with salvation: and her saints shall shout aloud for joy. There will I make the horn of David to bud: I have ordained a lamp for mine anointed. His enemies will I clothe with shame: but upon himself shall his crown flourish."

(Psalm 132:13-18)

What could be clearer? Everything revealed in Psalm 2 is repeated here: Zion promised as the place for his Father's name; the holy city; the people's needs satisfied with bread; his saints incorporated into the glory; the horn of David established, with Jesus himself being the promised horn; all his enemies vanquished. All this could be accomplished once the holy city was persuaded that his authority was from God in heaven. And so the temptation came to do the spectacular, to satisfy the people's curiosity once and for all time. Is it possible to reconstruct a thought process which possibly could give rise to the temptation forming in his mind?

If he were to do this thing, it would be a real wake-up call to the city and be the time of their redemption – for they were certain to accept him, surely? And with something as spectacular as casting off into the air, with no visible support or safety provisions, from the pinnacle some 150 feet above the temple courtyard – he couldn't fail to convince the people, could he?

From the psalm of David's true worship, the mind of Jesus could not fail to settle into the prophets with their descriptions of his work and messages of hope – particularly in the servant section of Isaiah:

"Awake, awake; put on thy strength, O Zion; put on thy beautiful garments, O Jerusalem, the holy city: for henceforth there shall no more come into thee the uncircumcised and the unclean." (Isaiah 52:1)

Jerusalem was identified as the holy city. Through him its salvation would come; no more oppressed or in bondage. This was the purpose of his coming, to bring hope and gently lead the people back to God. How straightforward to set it all in motion – he might have thought!

Other verses in this same Chapter 52 also speak of the fulfilment of God's eternal purpose of hope and comfort for the dying people. All these things would be made possible by the Arm of the Lord – and he was the Arm of the Lord, now made bare by his Father. All he did could only be to the honour and glory of his Father's name.

The pinnacle of the temple

Once Jesus had the vision of the holy city, he thought about the pinnacle. It was certainly the head of the corner. It towered far above the corner of the temple precinct wall – high and lifted up, and commanded a position of authority.

What did the scriptures say about "the head of the corner", being high and lifted up? Wasn't he the head of the corner? Hadn't Isaiah seen the vision of him, high and lifted up with his train filling the temple, and the whole earth full of his glory? (Isaiah 6:1,3). And were not the angels his train which would fill the temple and support him?

"The stone which the builders refused is become the head of the corner" (Psalm 118:22). His own disciple

Peter would in the future declare him to be "the head of the corner" (Acts 4:11 and 1 Peter 2:7). The refusal by the religious leaders as the builders, and this refusal taken up by the ordinary people as the labourers perhaps blindly or ignorantly, could be overcome, if only they could be persuaded that he was the Son of God, the head of the corner. The Gospel writers (Matthew 21:42, Mark 12:10, Luke 20:17), would record Jesus' declaration that he was the rejected stone, but also his claim that he was "the head of the corner", quoting the authority of Psalm 118.

The temple

Was not the temple the place where his Father said He would dwell? And had not Solomon, the type of the King in the glory of the kingdom of God, spoken of his Father, when he had said:

"I have built an house of habitation for thee, and a place for thy dwelling for ever ... But I have chosen Jerusalem that my name might be there."

(2 Chronicles 6:2,6)

All these things could come together in one moment of time as the Lord was transported in thought from the lonely wilderness to the holy city of Jerusalem. He could imagine the fulfilment of all things, and he had the power to hurry it along.

"If thou be the Son of God." Just as before there is the confident acceptance of himself as the Son of God. There was no doubt about this. The voice from heaven had declared it audibly and plainly: he was the Son of God. Yet his inner voice was setting up a challenge to his submission to the will of God, and the obedience he would offer as the sensitive and faithful Son, the servant of the Lord. It was cutting across all that he really wanted to be, all he needed to be for salvation's sake. But the voice was clear and deliberate.

"Cast thyself down"

He couldn't do this literally of course, for he was actually in the wilderness and not at the temple in Jerusalem,

90

whereas he could command stones into bread wherever he was. But the ground was being prepared so that this stunt could be attempted at any time during the ministry whenever he found himself in the temple precinct.

God's men in the past, in carrying forward the purpose had done spectacular events. A small stone had sunk the giant and his pride; the lions' mouths had been shut; there was no smell of fire or scorch on the three friends; city walls had fallen when trumpets sounded; the sun stood still for a whole day; enemies were defeated by holding up a rod or a spear; water gushed out of the rock when struck. What was so different about jumping off a high pinnacle?

There then follows in the temptation narratives of both Matthew (4:6) and Luke (4:10), the passage from Psalm 91, prefaced by "it is written". It is a psalm that confirms and promises certain things on certain conditions.

Angelic help

"For he shall give his angels charge over thee, to keep thee in all thy ways. They shall bear thee up in their hands, lest thou dash thy foot against a stone."

(Psalm 91:11,12)

This is a wonderful promise of angelic help and support. We know from our own reading and possibly our experience that angels really do provide this kind of help and protection. We may have personal stories to tell of events in our lives.

But here in clear prophetic language is the confirmation that Jesus too would get all the support and care he needed, "in all his ways", to fulfil the ministry allotted to him. Jesus' life was in the hands of heavenly beings with unlimited power – what more could he want!

His early life had been miraculously preserved by angelic involvement. An angel had first spoken to his mother and arranged his conception; one had overseen his growth in the womb; an innumerable company had praised God in song at his birth; one had given a message of hope to Joseph about the honour of husbands in family life; there had been the flight into Egypt to avoid the massacre of the innocents; he had been protected during his time in the temple, aged twelve years, when he was missing for three days from the returning pilgrim party to Nazareth. At the end of the forty days of temptation angels would minister again.

What else does the psalm tell us about the Father and Son relationship?

"Thou shalt tread upon the lion and adder: the young lion and the dragon shalt thou trample under feet. Because he hath set his love upon me, therefore will I deliver him: I will set him on high, because he hath known my name. He shall call upon me, and I will answer him: I will be with him in trouble; I will deliver him, and honour him. With long life will I satisfy him, and show him my salvation."

(Psalm 91:13-16)

In verse 13 there is the reference to the "wild beasts" of Mark's temptation account, Jesus' overcoming and having dominion over them, and of those beasts losing their ferocity in the presence of the King. There are clear allusions to Genesis 3:15, Psalm 8:6-8, Deuteronomy 8:15 and Genesis 1:26.

In verse 14 we have the words, "He hath set his love upon me". This is the assurance of the Father about His devoted Son – and he had.

Again, "I will set him on high" is the great promise of deliverance from death and exaltation to kingdom glory.

At verse 15 is the Father's promise to respond positively when His Son called and said he was in difficulty, or just needed to be comforted and strengthened; and He would deliver him from all kinds of terror and evil, until finally in verse 16 the promised gift of eternal life will be granted, through resurrection out of the dead.

All these things Jesus knew. He had read the words before; he believed them. They were part of, "every word that proceedeth out of the mouth of the LORD doth man live". This was his story; he was living it. These words and promises were specifically for him, for his comfort as well as his instruction. Jesus had engaged with the teaching and knew that his life was secured and protected in the secret places and under the shadow. He would not be harmed.

9

IS THE LORD AMONG US OR NOT?

THE tempter said, "He shall give his angels charge over thee, to keep thee" (Luke 4:10), whereas the Psalmist had said, "For he shall give his angels charge over thee, to keep thee *in all thy ways*". The italicised words are the crucial ones. These are omitted from the gospel records of the temptation as the following table shows, implying that they were not part of the 'conversation' or the thinking process, when the thought about the pinnacle event first became alive in the mind of Jesus.

Psalm 91:11,12 "For he shall give his angels charge over thee, to keep thee in all thy ways. They shall bear thee up in their hands, lest thou dash thy foot against a stone."			
Phrase in the Psalm	**Matthew 4:6**	**Luke 4:10,11**	**LXX of Psalm text**
"To keep thee"	Omitted (from AV/RV)	Included (in AV/RV)	included
"In all thy ways"	Omitted (from AV/RV)	Omitted (from AV/RV)	included
"At any time" (omitted from AV/RV)	Included (in AV/RV – added from LXX)	Included (in AV/RV – added from LXX)	included

Inaccurate scriptures?

Why does the text of the Old Testament include these words, confirmed by the Septuagint Greek Translation, but the New Testament omit them? Is the quotation of the Old Testament made by the tempter appropriate? If not, it's an example of the improper use of scripture. Yet the appeal was to a spirit of trustfulness that had stood the Lord in good stead on the earlier occasion.

Is it possible that the mind of Jesus was playing tricks, given his probable dehydrated and hungry physical condition? This may seem a strange and almost blasphemous thing to say of our Lord Jesus, but we are attempting to explore the reasons for, and the difficulties of, the temptations. We must bear in mind that, "The heart of man is deceitful above all things and desperately wicked". If this is so, it would have been a stumbling block, an offence, an assertion of the flesh. The question was, 'In whose ways would he be kept, and why?'

The answer, obviously, is in the ways of the Spirit, the ways of God. As long as Jesus walked in the ways of God, with his perfect heart, and his focus fixed on the fulfilment of his Father's will, he was in the right way and the promise was clear – that he would be 'kept'. But Jesus was being tempted to express the ways of the flesh and deny God. Certainly the Father would keep His Son in all spiritual ways, but possibly not if gross foolishness was entered into wilfully and deliberately, and if he set himself in opposition against God's ways.

If he accepted the prompt to cast himself down, if he offered no defence and did not find fault with the idea put by the tempter, that would create doubt about his integrity and loyalty to God. It would also challenge the authority of his Father. If he were to "yield [his] members as instruments of unrighteousness unto sin", even just this once, his perfect relationship with his Father would be marred. It would be so much easier the next time he faced a similar situation, to deny his

95

Father's authority and please himself. Such situations would arise many times in the days and months ahead.

But by then it wouldn't really matter whether he was obedient or not, for the purpose of God which was settled in him would already be frustrated. He could not be the Lamb without blemish that would take away the sin of the world. He could not expect to defeat sin, for sin had already conquered him. The battle would be lost and over.

Also, to do such a thing, for the reasons imagined, would be to challenge his support by the angels of God. It is true they are ministering spirits sent forth to minister to the heirs of salvation, and what greater heir of salvation could there be than the Lord Jesus? The affairs of this world are in the hands of the angels. It is possible of course that the angels would have been charged concerning him, and they would have borne him up in their hands, lest he dashed his foot against a stone.

But what was being considered, to cast himself down from the pinnacle, was presumptuous and therefore wrong. Although the promise had been made that he could in faith rely on the angels, they were still his Father's ministers, to do his Father's pleasure, for they hearkened to the voice of his Father's word (Psalm 103:20,21). To engage in the spectacular and do a stunt to satisfy those who would demand a sign from heaven was self-centred. It was not the right way to convince his people of their needs. His Father had decreed that it was to be the word of life in its simplicity and preaching that would convict men's hearts and minds of sin, and help them to turn to God in repentance for spiritual healing.

So a counter-scripture is quoted to oppose the devilish use of God's word – "It is written again, Thou shalt not tempt the Lord thy God".

"It is written again"

Before we think about the answer Jesus gave, let us just consider the phrase, "It is written". There is a force and an authority in these words. It is the equivalent of "God said", and when God spoke, it was done. We have already looked at one aspect of this in chapter 4.

In Luke's account of the temptation at 4:12, Jesus is recorded as saying, "It is said". This means 'It is written'. There is no difference between the original spoken word, and the subsequent written word, as it all carries equal authority from God. Take for example the creation account of Genesis 1, the repetitive words, "and God said", and the things that happened in response to this command. Is this not part of "every word that proceedeth out of the mouth of the LORD" by which man shall live? Without these creative acts there would be no life on earth as we know and enjoy it. Or again:

> "By the word of the LORD were the heavens made;
> and all the host of them by the breath of his mouth ...
> For he spake, and it was done; he commanded, and it
> stood fast." (Psalm 33:6,9)

Note, "word of the LORD", "breath of his mouth", "he spake", "he commanded". We can see the connection between these four phrases. It is the authoritative voice of God, the word from God, acting to accomplish His will, for the simple reason, "God said".

> "The LORD said unto my Lord, Sit thou at my right
> hand, until I make thine enemies thy footstool."
> (Psalm 110:1)

This is a prophetic Messianic psalm for Yahweh said that Christ's enemies would be his footstool. It was a promise pertinent to Jesus' present situation in the wilderness as he struggled with the temptations. One of the questions to be answered was, 'Do I push on with this spectacular now, or do I defer to my Father's will and His good time'? The promise would be fulfilled but it needed an obedient and faithful Son, who was totally devoted to his Father's purpose, to ensure that the enemies would be his footstool.

Jesus answers the temptation

Jesus' answer to the tempter's 'misquotation' from Psalm 91 is found in the words of Deuteronomy 6:

> "Ye shall not tempt the LORD your God, as ye tempted him in Massah"   (verse 16)

Why does Jesus refer to the events at Massah? Why is this text appropriate to his situation? The following table helps us see the context of Deuteronomy 6.

v. 1	God's expectations of the people and the sure promise of the land.
vv. 2,3	The responsibility of the Children of Israel – to observe and do the commandments and to fear the Lord.
vv. 4,5	The unity of God – to love and to fear Him with all the heart and mind.
vv. 6,7	The unity of God – the responsibility to absorb the word of God and to teach the next generation the same law.
vv. 8,9	The unity of God – emphasis on talk, talk, and more talk about the word of God.
vv. 10,11	The promised land with its great and goodly cities was well stocked with a productive earth. Jerusalem will be established there.
v. 12	Do not forget God or your previous bondage and release.
vv. 13,14	Worship the only One God when in the land – ignore the idols and gods of the nations.
vv. 15	The one and only God is a jealous God – He can be angry and provoked.
vv. 16	Therefore do not tempt the Lord your God, as at Massah.

These points serve to emphasise the certainty of the care and the presence of God, and His involvement in the lives of the Children of Israel as a nation and individually, and also in the life of Jesus. This is the reassurance that God was among them, as He was with Jesus. He had done great things for them, and He looked for a corresponding and faithful response as a thanksgiving for His generosity and kindness.

Events at Massah

This brings us to Massah. What happened here that Moses should need to refer to it again after forty years? The account of the rebellion is in Exodus 17.

In passing we note that the temptation to command stones into bread is rooted in Exodus 16. This is about God's miraculous provision of manna on a daily basis, which continued for forty years without fail, until the Children of Israel crossed over the Jordan under Joshua. The daily supply of manna began in the Wilderness of Sin, between Elim and Sinai.

In Exodus 17, the people had moved on to Rephidim, a place which had no water. Had God forgotten or overlooked that there was no water there, neither wells nor rivers? Was God uninterested in the people's welfare? Of course not!

He knew there was no water, and as the angel directed the journeying of the children of Israel, so He deliberately brought them to this place. It was part of the humbling, proving, affliction and straitness, to know what was in their hearts, mentioned in Deuteronomy 8. It was a trial of their faith, a test of their confidence in the goodness and the word of God.

> "Wherefore the people did chide with Moses, and said, Give us water that we may drink. And Moses said unto them, Why chide ye with me? wherefore do ye tempt the LORD?" (Exodus 17:2)

Here is the challenge, the rebellion. To "chide" is to wrangle, to grapple, and to hold a controversy. It seems like a contest of strength. But it is also tempting the

99

Lord God by putting Him to the test, proving Him, and provoking Him to provide water because they did not believe that He cared, nor did they understand what was going on.

In verse 3 they "murmur", that is they complain, hold a grudge, and are obstinate, and by implication it can mean 'to stay permanently'. Does this mean the Children of Israel were not prepared to move on and would have returned to Egypt? Possibly. But it could be they continually murmured and complained to Moses about what they perceived as God's lack of interest in them, as they endured the hardships of Rephidim and elsewhere. There was open unbelief about God's purpose of redemption. This same complaint had been made about the lack of bread in Exodus 16:3, but God had provided it, and they had been filled, and silenced for the time being. They were to learn that speaking evil of the rulers was speaking evil of God Himself. They were in a blame culture.

In Exodus 17:4 the people prepared to stone Moses as he was the one they saw as responsible for their predicament. To provide a remedy and relief from their thirst, Moses and the elders of Israel as witnesses, were instructed to go forward to Horeb. The angel stood on the rock. Moses struck the rock once, and fresh life-giving water poured out. Jesus would understand it as a figure of his own life-giving death.

"And he called the name of the place Massah, and Meribah, because of the chiding of the children of Israel, and because they tempted the LORD, saying, Is the LORD among us, or not?" (Exodus 17:7)

The question the people asked encapsulated their murmuring and dissatisfaction with Moses and with God: "Is the LORD among us, or not?" This was the pinnacle of unfaithfulness and a denial of the very nature of God and His everlasting promises; and of all the evidences they had seen in the miracles, wonders and signs which had been done on their behalf.

Does God exist?

The people's question was challenging. Did God really exist? Did He really care? Did He really govern the world? Was He as good as His word? This was all a distrust of God and His word and works generally, yet did not take into account all the benefits they had received in the previous six weeks, including the daily supply of manna. They had collected it that very morning! But they had sadly forgotten who had provided it. This was tantamount to utter disbelief in God, His power, His foreknowledge, His providential care, His creative qualities to give life and sustain it. Their attitude was rebellious and sinful.

It is this attitude of rebelliousness that Jesus referred to when answering and denying the second temptation to do the spectacular, however persuasive and triumphant it could have been. Ironically Moses did just that when he struck the rock and there was a positive and good result! Water gushed out and the people's thirst was satisfied. Sadly there is no clue in the divine record that they answered their own question, with a resounding 'Yes!' for the next event was war with Amalek.

"Is the LORD among us or not?" This was the question Jesus might have asked himself in the desperate moments when the temptation came to cast himself down from the pinnacle. The answer is of course, 'Yes, the Lord is among us'. Jesus could say, 'Yes He is with me, as He was with my fathers, as He has promised never to leave me or forsake me'. Therefore he would resist the temptation. He had not been deserted; the Father was close.

Tempting God

"Wherefore do ye tempt the LORD?" Moses had challenged in Exodus 17:2. The New Testament is explicit:

> "Let no man say when he is tempted, I am tempted of God: for God cannot be tempted with evil, neither tempteth he any man." (James 1:13)

Had Moses got it wrong when he said in the confusion of the moment, 'Why do you tempt the Lord?' There is

101

no conflict of course. James had said, "God cannot be tempted with evil", worthless things, but He can be provoked to anger and judgement by manifest disbelief, especially when He has demonstrated the care by which He sustains and protects. This is the Old Testament equivalent of "blasphemy against the Holy Spirit", denying the power and authority of God, or what the Old Testament itself called "vexing his holy Spirit" (Isaiah 63:10).

Ultimately of course, all sin and rebellion is against God. David in Psalm 51 discovered this after his wicked behaviour with Bathsheba and confessed, "Against thee, thee only, have I sinned, and done this evil in thy sight" (verse 4): not that Bathsheba or Uriah had not been sinned against, for clearly they had, but because only God Himself is holy and righteous, abundant in goodness and truth, and the ultimate standard in morality. As Jesus said, "There is none good but one, that is God". David was God's appointed ruler; he had received gifts and graces beyond compare, had been protected and strengthened in his fugitive years and in battle, and was in a deep personal fellowship with God. These things brought grave responsibilities as well as privileges.

Similarly, in the New Testament, when Peter in Acts 5 addressed the satanic thoughts and lies in the hearts of Ananias and Sapphira, he concluded his judgement by asking, "How is it that ye have agreed together to tempt the Spirit of the Lord?" (verse 9). Both Ananias and Sapphira, like Peter himself, were called individually to the Gospel. They had been baptized and had entered into a personal and precious covenant of love, with all its responsibilities of faith. Coupled with this were the privileges of fellowship in the community of God's called out people, destined for great things in the ages to come. To cheat the ecclesia of God was denying the Lord that bought them. So all sin is against God, for eventually all succumb to mortality and all come under His condemnation.

The second answer of Jesus

Let us continue to explore the text of Deuteronomy 6 where Jesus' rebuttal of this temptation came from.

v. 17	Diligently keep the commandments – this would include the purpose of his baptism.
v. 18	Do what is right and good before God, anticipating "I come … to do thy will, O my God" in Psalm 40, to secure the occupation of the land.
v. 19	"To *cast out* all thine enemies", and the last enemy is death, the main barrier to perfect fellowship with God. But the immediate enemy is diabolical thoughts; they must be cast down and cast out.
v. 20	*When a Son* asks, "What mean the testimonies?", Jesus would know he was the Son referred to.
vv. 21-23	The answer is that bondmen were freed from Egypt with great signs and wonders, by a gracious God who led them hitherto with a promise of a kingdom to come.
v. 24	It is always for the children's good to preserve them alive – Jesus was the chosen child.
v. 25	Accounted righteous if the commands are observed and done – the promise was for Jesus especially.

These verses are a statement about the faithfulness of the son who was called out of Egypt, and the promise of a long life in a good land. In return, the people covenanted to be true and keep the commandments and the testimonies, which were written and provided for their good. They would be victorious in their warfare

103

and the generations to come would be preserved alive. Nothing could stem the flow of mercy, kindness and grace from God, if they themselves were honourable. As the true Son, Jesus knew that what was written aforetime was written for him and about him.

Therefore, do not "tempt the Lord thy God", as He was tempted earlier at the place Moses called Massah when the Children of Israel were just about forty days out of Egypt.

The 'misquotation' by the tempter from Psalm 91 mentioned earlier introduced false teaching into the equation. It was a delusion. The deception could have led Jesus to a place where there was no assurance or promise of safety from the Lord. The spectacular event would bring instant popularity but for the wrong reasons. Therefore putting God to the test to see if He would deny His own righteous judgements and principles, to save His Son from self-willed action, was misplaced faith as well as deliberate and foolhardy. Therefore, "Ye shall not tempt the LORD your God". Certainly not, especially when angelic beings were to be involved in the proposed spectacular event. The temptation was successfully repulsed.

The Lord's attitude is revealed in Psalm 91:

"He that dwelleth in the secret place of the most High shall abide under the shadow of the Almighty. I will say of the LORD, He is my refuge and my fortress: my God; in him will I trust."   (verses 1,2)

This is an expression of God's faithfulness and the richness of His fellowship to those who choose to be close to Him. Jesus was living just as verse 1 describes. God was his refuge and hiding place. He did all this, and there was a secure daily abiding. He did trust. He had learned the patience needed. The rest of the psalm confirms the close relationship enjoyed between the Father and Son. But he knew his greater purpose was described in verses 13-16:

Verse 13 – he must tread on serpents to defeat sin.

Verse 14 – his love had been given and received, so deliverance was sure.

Verse 14 – his setting on high and being exalted, required the cross first.

Verse 15 – answers would come to comfort and deliver him even at the moment of temptation and trouble.

Verse 16 – long life and salvation was the ultimate answer and the completion of his Father's will, but not yet.

We can draw our own conclusions from this testing examination of our Lord:

1. That presumptuous dependence is folly and wrong, for it is provoking God to act against all His revealed principles of what is just and true and good.

2. That the care of God is certain – but in His own time and for His glory, and no flesh can or should glory in His presence.

3. That angels would minister and support him – as events in the Garden of Gethsemane and at the tomb subsequently proved – but meanwhile they are provided as and when needed.

The Father was aware of all His Son's circumstances, fears and concerns. He would not test him beyond his capacity, but with the temptations He made ways of escape so that Jesus was able, not merely to bear them, but utterly and ultimately to defeat them.

Thanks be to God!

10

ALL THE KINGDOMS OF THE WORLD

IN introducing this third temptation Matthew uses the word "again":

"Again, the devil taketh him up into an exceeding high mountain, and showeth him all the kingdoms of the world, and the glory of them."   (Matthew 4:8)

We also note in verse 5 the word "then" and in verse 3, "when". "When ... then ... again". There appears to be a progression and regularity about these temptations; as if they had occurred more than once and kept repeating during the forty days and nights of the wilderness sojourn. Perhaps there was a continuous repetition of temptations which is being suggested by the use of these words. It would be difficult to argue that no temptation whatsoever occurred before the near expiry of the forty days, and it was only these three right at the end of the period which came to test Jesus.

Bullinger suggests that because Matthew and Luke each record three temptations but in a different order, there must have been six main temptations altogether – two of each of the three kinds.[1] He deduces this on the basis that the introductory words to each of the three temptations are different, as are the three conversations between Jesus and the tempter. In connection with this third temptation, "the kingdoms of the world", Bullinger argues that the order of the words in verse 8 should be, 'The devil taketh him again', implying that he had taken him there before and this was a repetition, in the same way as, "It is written again" in verse 7. Whatever we think of this idea, it goes some way to prop up a view

1   *The Companion Bible*, Appendix 116, page 156, "The Temptations of our Lord".

of continuous temptations throughout the forty days and nights.

But perhaps these three temptations were the most difficult to deal with, or the most subtle, or simply the summation of all that temptation is. I am personally inclined to this latter view. In other words, *all* temptation can be classified under one of these three kinds. This is confirmed in 1 John 2:

> "For all that is in the world, the lust of the flesh, and the lust of the eyes, and the pride of life, is not of the Father, but is of the world."   (verse 16)

We conclude that it means Jesus was tested and tried many times during his wilderness period, in a variety of ways, as well as in the three very specific ways at the end.

The devil

It is worth noting that Matthew uses the term 'devil' on four occasions, and 'Satan' once; and Luke uses 'devil' five times and 'Satan' once.

The devil (Greek, *ho diabolos*) is the false accuser; the slanderer; the evil one; the adversary. It is a figure of speech for all that is in opposition to God (see the earlier section headed, "The tempter" with a table of Gospel words).

The term is used of the law or principle that is in our members; it is our genetic disposition to wrongdoing, so making us mortal, as well as being 'le provocateur' of the individual sins we commit. The same law was at work in Jesus. The conflicts between Jesus and the tempter, and the debates in deciding whether to agree or to resist what was being suggested by the 'devil', were all going on in the mind of Jesus. The mind is the battleground for all of us. Jesus was able to conquer on each occasion. But that did not prevent either good or less worthy thoughts beginning in, or entering the mind of Jesus, however rapidly he disposed of the unhelpful ones.

107

Exceeding high mountain

The Gospels of Matthew and Luke record that this temptation took place in "an exceeding high mountain", and Luke adds that the kingdoms were shown "in a moment of time". But there is no "exceeding high mountain" in Judaea or the wildernesses of Israel. The highest mountain in Israel is Mount Hermon in the north at 9,232 feet (2,814 m), which is twice as high as Ben Nevis in Scotland (highest mountain in the UK), but only one third the height of Mount Everest at 29,000 feet (8,840 m) approximately. But Jesus was not up a mountain, however high – he was in the wilderness. Jesus would be able to see from the wilderness where these temptations were taking place to the surrounding mountainous horizons, on which the sun would shine and reflect creating confusing patterns of light and dark, shapes and shadow. The very shape of the distant barren peaks of these lonely mountain tops in this unfriendly and hostile environment suggested the pinnacle of the temple, which was the 'location' of the second temptation, and where Jesus was transported in mind but not in body.

In any event it would be impossible to see "all the kingdoms of the world in a moment of time", even from the highest spot on earth due to the circle of the earth. Therefore a literal understanding of a mountain location of this third temptation is unhelpful. This image is taking shape in the mind of Jesus as he considers his kingship, and all the promises and prophecies made about him in relation to the kingdom.

All the kingdoms of the world

Jesus was shown "all the kingdoms of the world in a moment of time" by the devil. Let us just reflect for one moment. Who had seen all the kingdoms of the world from a high mountain – that is, all the kingdoms that really mattered?

Abraham is probably the first to be granted the vision of 'all the kingdom'.

"And the LORD said unto Abram, after that Lot was separated from him, Lift up now thine eyes, and look from the place where thou art northward, and southward, and eastward and westward: for all the land which thou seest, to thee will I give it, and to thy seed for ever ... Arise, walk through the land in the length of it and in the breadth of it; for I will give it unto thee."   (Genesis 13:14,15,17)

It is reasonable to assume that Abraham was between Bethel and Ai (verse 3) when this promise was made. Just two miles north of Bethel is the highest spot in the centre of the land at 3,332 feet (1,016 m). From here Abraham could have seen as far as Dan in the north, Beersheba in the south, to the Mediterranean Sea in the west and the Dead Sea in the east. He was shown the whole land from the highest point and then invited to walk it.

Moses perhaps on the day of his death was also shown 'the kingdoms of the world':

"And Moses went up to the plains of Moab unto the mountain of Nebo, to the top of Pisgah, that is over against Jericho. And the LORD showed him all the land of Gilead, unto Dan, and all Naphtali, and the land of Ephraim, and Manasseh, and all the land of Judah, unto the utmost sea, and the south, and the plain of the valley of Jericho, the city of palm trees, unto Zoar."   (Deuteronomy 34:1-3)

Moses was in Mount Nebo which is about 2,630 feet (802 m) and situated on the east bank of the River Jordan. From this vantage point he was able to see across the Jordan Valley, west as far as the Mediterranean Sea at sixty-five miles (105 km) distance; eighty miles (129 km) south beyond Beersheba; and to the north he could see Dan at 105 miles (169 km). He could see as far as this because "his eye was not dim, nor his natural force abated" (verse 7) even at 120 years old. He had seen the kingdom but could not enter.

So it was not impossible to be shown the heart of the kingdom of God in a moment of time – but not all the

109

kingdoms of the world of men, that is of the Roman habitable or the Roman world of the first century, at least not literally or physically, for the one simple reason that the kingdoms of men at the time of Jesus extended well beyond the boundaries of the promised land.

The patriarchs had seen the reality of the promises of God; the land really existed. The specific seed to inherit this was the Lord Jesus Christ himself. This was the kingdom which mattered to Jesus. Was not the image he was forming, the initiative to make the promises real for himself?

The temptation

"And the devil said unto him, All this power will I give thee, and the glory of them: for that is delivered unto me; and to whomsoever I will I give it. If thou therefore wilt worship me, all shall be thine."

(Luke 4:6,7)

The first thing to note is that the power being offered is the authority and rulership over all the kingdoms of the world and that Jesus himself would be the King. All this was promised. The scriptures spoke clearly about it: Jesus knew he was to be the King.

But on offer were the physical, literal, mortal, evil, corrupt kingdoms of a world which would pass away; not the purified, holy, cleansed, spiritually-based and future kingdom which is destined to last forever and which was the subject of the promises made to the fathers of the nation. This was a personal goal of Jesus still to be accomplished by self-sacrifice and devotion to the will of his Father. The devil was not giving away power over this future kingdom, only those human kingdoms and nations which existed then. Yet even the kingdom of God is to be a physical, literal, land-based kingdom centred on the land where Jesus was.

This temptation is about "the lust of the eyes". It is presented in the words of scripture referring to kingdoms and kingship, and this would make it sound credible, especially when coupled with the associated power and glory. When the devil put before Jesus the possibility of power, authority and the glory of the kingdom, he showed him "all the kingdoms of the world". To have received them by capitulation to the devil's temptation would have been covetous, and "covetousness ... is idolatry" (Colossians 3:5), and therefore sinful.

To satisfy "the lust of the eyes" would have displaced God from His rightful position as the Lord of the Universe, and put in place other interests, other gods, other goals. It would have set aside the one true God who then could not be worshipped with all the heart, soul, strength and mind. The Lord God no longer has the first place; He has been deposed as the rightful Master and another has replaced Him.

There is an interesting omission in the account of this third temptation. When *diabolos* spoke on an earlier occasion, to tempt Jesus to jump off the pinnacle of the temple, the words "it is written" were used to disguise as authentic the temptation that was on offer. They gave credence to the test, and to the unwary would make it seem quite genuine and without guile. But this time, there is no "it is written"; instead a collection of different texts which gave the invitation the same apparent substance and authenticity. Additionally, there is no reference either to "if thou be the Son of God". Sonship was certain, without question and fully accepted.

Luke's account appears to be a reasoning process which is taking place in the mind of Jesus about his own future, what he had been promised and would inherit. It seems that Jesus had considered the whole of his life and its purpose, and raced on to the future promised for the faithful Son and servant. It would have frustrated the purpose of God if Jesus had taken control of the kingdoms of the world at that time, as the temptation is about foiling his mission to be the suffering servant of God.

Scripture can support many times over every phrase in Luke's record of the 'offer' which was put to Jesus. The *diabolos* had brought together on this occasion a collection of evidence that could justify his claim to kingship – not just from one source but from across the whole of scripture, particularly the psalms and the prophets.

In all the scriptures

"The devil ... showed unto him all the kingdoms of the world in a moment of time. And the devil said unto him, All this power will I give thee, and the glory of them: for that is delivered unto me; and to whomsoever I will I give it." (Luke 4:5,6)

These verses consist of four main ideas. We shall examine these four parts separately, looking at a few of the possible passages which seem appropriate as the following table shows. The reason for doing this is to confirm that on the face of it the way the scripture was presented in the temptation is legitimate and its content true.

The 'tempting' phrases	Possible Old Testament references
"All the kingdoms of the world."	Genesis 1:26, and Genesis 13,15,17,22. Psalms 8, 24, 72. Daniel 2 and 7:13,14.
"All this power will I give thee, and the glory of them."	1 Chronicles 29:11. Psalm 63:1,2; 145:10-13.
"For that is delivered unto me."	Psalm 2:6-9 and Psalms 87, 89, 110, 132. 1 Chronicles 17:11-14. Ezekiel 21:27.
"To whomsoever I will I give it."	Daniel 4:17; 5:21; 7:22,27.

"All the kingdoms of the world"

"I saw in the night visions, and, behold, one like the Son of man came with the clouds of heaven, and came to the Ancient of days, and they brought him near before him. And there was given him dominion, and glory, and a kingdom, that all people, nations, and languages, should serve him: his dominion is an everlasting dominion, which shall not pass away, and his kingdom that which shall not be destroyed."

(Daniel 7:13,14)

We note the emphasis on dominion, kingdom, peoples and nations – an everlasting dominion and the indestructible kingdom; also the reference to "glory" and the links with the next phrase of the 'invitation'. As indicated above, similar passages could have been chosen from Psalms 8, 24, and 72 or Daniel 2 and 2 Samuel 7, or Genesis 13, 15, 17 and 22 and many more, in order to demonstrate the thoroughness of the teaching in the Old Testament and the consistency of the inspired writers of scripture about the kingdoms of men becoming the future kingdom of God.

"All this power will I give thee, and the glory of them"

There are at least three places in the Old Testament where 'power' and 'glory' come together. We shall examine the two from the Psalms, but 1 Chronicles 29:11 is equally powerful in demonstrating the Lord's kingdom authority.

'O God, thou art my God; early will I seek thee: my soul thirsteth for thee, my flesh longeth for thee in a dry and thirsty land, where no water is; to see thy power and thy glory, so as I have seen thee in the sanctuary." (Psalm 63:1,2)

The wilderness setting of this prayer-psalm, and the desire to see the power and glory of the Father translated into the promised kingdom, would be very pertinent to the Lord Jesus in his wilderness temptations. Here was a way to finish the trials and assume the promised glory. But would it be right? The rest of the psalm would answer the question.

"All thy works shall praise thee, O LORD; and thy saints shall bless thee. They shall speak of the glory of thy kingdom, and talk of thy power; to make known to the sons of men his mighty acts, and the glorious majesty of his kingdom. Thy kingdom is an everlasting kingdom, and thy dominion endureth throughout all generations."　　　(Psalm 145:10-13)

This is a description of the fullness of the kingdom with its associated glory and power, and joy at the inclusion of others, both saints and sons of men in this everlasting dominion. If ever there was a positive hopeful psalm that expressed all the anticipated joys of the kingdom age, with its benefits for downtrodden peoples, this is it. It tells of the Father's kindness and how His hand is extended to the needy and the faithful. The question that might have been asked is, 'Surely it must be right to bring about this good and generous age – even now?'

"That is delivered unto me"

"I will overturn, overturn, overturn, it: and it shall be no more, until he come whose right it is; and I will give it him."　　　(Ezekiel 21:27)

This must be one of the clearest messages in the whole of the Old Testament, that the kingdom of Israel will be delivered to the Lord Jesus Christ, as the rightful heir of the vacant throne. For long ages the prophets of God had declared that the seed of Abraham and the Son of David was the designated King of the world-dominating kingdom. Jesus will reign as king – that was promised!

"Yet have I set my king on my holy hill of Zion. I will declare the decree: the LORD hath said unto me, Thou art my Son; this day have I begotten thee. Ask of me, and I shall give thee the heathen for thine inheritance, and the uttermost parts of the earth for thy possession. Thou shalt break them with a rod of iron; thou shalt dash them in pieces like a potter's vessel."　　　(Psalm 2:6-9)

114

We note the direct references to the king, the holy hill, the given inheritance of all the earth as the everlasting possession; and ultimately the mighty ruler with unlimited authority and power. This is equally one of the plainest declarations by God that His Son would be able to execute all power and judgement in the earth. This is exactly what the people of God desperately needed: freedom from the dominating Roman bondage, and good spiritual leadership to bring them back to true worship and the honour of a holy God. And now the opportunity was presenting itself, so that the age old promises could be realised.

We can take just one incident from the ministry of Jesus, and it shows his understanding of his kingship and that this knowledge was most certainly in his mind even at the time of the temptation:

> "All things are delivered unto me of my Father: and no man knoweth the Son, but the Father; neither knoweth any man the Father, save the Son, and he to whomsoever the Son will reveal him."
>
> (Matthew 11:27)

There are parallels here with the temptation passages, particularly the first and last phrases of this verse: "All things are delivered unto me", and "He to whom the Son will reveal him". Note also the oblique link with the next phrase of the temptation. The parallel passage in Luke 10:22 includes a marginal note that, "Many ancient copies add these words, 'And turning to his disciples, he said'". So it seems that Jesus was making a definitive statement about his role in the purpose of God and its subsequent fulfilment, and that the disciples too could have a part. They had received their revelation from the Son himself.

"To whomsoever I will I give it"

The prophet Daniel had declared to Nebuchadnezzar that "the most High ruleth in the kingdom of men". This was by the authority of the watchers and the holy ones, that is the angels, who have in their care and under their jurisdiction this present world, the kingdoms of men. They are given into the hands of whoever will serve the purpose of God best, whether he is a good man, or the basest of men. Ultimately the kingdoms of men will become the kingdoms of our Lord and of his Christ (Revelation 11:15). So there should be no problem in transferring this prophecy to Christ, as (i) all authority has been given to him (John 5:19-23), and (ii) he has the name above every other name (Philippians 2:9-11).

> "... until the Ancient of days came, and judgment was given to the saints of the most High; and the time came that the saints possessed the kingdom ... And the kingdom and dominion, and the greatness of the kingdom under the whole heaven, shall be given to the people of the saints of the most High, whose kingdom is an everlasting kingdom, and all dominions shall serve and obey him."
>
> (Daniel 7:22,27)

How closely this patterns the thrust of the tempter's inviting offer: 'Worship me – all is yours – take the kingdoms of the world – give them to who you want'. All this was promised. Jesus knew he was to be the King of the world in the age to come. But the whole force of this temptation was, 'Take it all now, it's yours for the asking, it's been promised to you. Share it with your friends. Just be what you are destined to be. Why wait?'

The scriptures which were incorporated into this final temptation were direct and decisive. They were positive, definite, sure and powerful. They stated in unequivocal language that the kingdoms of the world are to become the kingdoms of our Lord and of his Christ. The kingdoms of the world were his for the taking – weren't they?

The mind of the serpent

Whilst it is true that the scripture references, brought together in the way they were, on the surface appear sound in making their overall teaching plausible, the thinking behind the spoken word of the tempter was devilish and exactly how the serpent hooked Eve in

Genesis 3. The serpent's initial approach was to speak the truth and present the facts. It was Eve who answered inadequately and carelessly. She did not remind herself or the serpent of the exact words the angel and Adam had spoken, when the commandment to avoid the tree of the knowledge of good and evil was first made to her. The serpent then spoke the lie, but quickly passed on to another true statement about the consequences of eating fruit from the tree of the knowledge of good and evil. Eve did not take in *all* the serpent had said, and proceeded to consider the forbidden fruit as an attractive and alternative proposition.

This is what the *diabolos* was doing in this third temptation. The general invitation is couched in sound scripture which was well known and true. It was quickly followed up by the temptation, and even half of this was true: "all shall be thine"!

Wrong thinking

But the means to that end were spurious – If thou wilt fall down and worship me". This was the heart of the matter. But it was deceptive; it was false thinking. The kingdoms of the world are transient (1 John 2:17) even though they appear to be 'forever' and age-lasting. There was a serious flaw in this devilish thinking of the flesh, in the way the 'offer' of kingdom inheritance was put, as the following table shows.

The kingdoms were not Jesus' to take – they are in the gift of God (Psalm 2:8; John 6:37).
The present world belongs to God – even the cattle on a thousand hills (Psalm 50:9-14).
Seeking the glory without the cross, sacrifice and resurrection would not be true and would not last.
Taking the glory to himself was not acknowledging God as all in all (1 Corinthians 15:27,28).

117

Self-worship is the exaltation of human pride – not acceptable to God (Proverbs 6:16-19).
There was the danger of forgetting where the honour of the kingdom came from (Deuteronomy 8:17-19).

"And thou say in thine heart, My power and the might of mine hand hath gotten me this wealth. But thou shalt remember the LORD thy God: for it is he that giveth thee power to get wealth, that he may establish his covenant which he sware unto thy fathers, as it is this day. And it shall be, if thou do at all forget the LORD thy God, and walk after other gods, and serve them, and worship them, I testify against you this day that ye shall surely perish."
(Deuteronomy 8:17-19)

This was the issue lodging briefly in his human heart. The thinking was dangerous, because "the heart is deceitful above all things, and desperately sick". And Jesus knew it.

The answer

The answer to this dilemma was quickly recognised and grappled with: "Get thee hence, Satan" (Matthew 4:10, but omitted in Luke 4:8, RV) and "It is written". The problem was addressed head on.

"Thou shalt fear the Lord thy God, and him only shalt thou serve; and thou shalt cleave to him, and by his name thou shalt swear. Go ye not after other gods of the gods of the nations round about you; for the Lord thy God in the midst of thee is a jealous God, lest the Lord thy God be very angry with thee, and destroy thee from off the face of the earth."
(Deuteronomy 6:13-15, LXX)

We note the additional words: "thou shalt cleave to him", and which are repeated in Deuteronomy 10:20.

In this verse 13, "fear" (Old Testament) becomes "worship" (New Testament), and means to revere, to be had in reverence, to be paid honour and respect. 'Serve him' links with the first and second commandments of Deuteronomy 5:7-9 and repeated in Deuteronomy 6:4-6, with the emphasis on loving the Lord God with *all* of the heart, soul, mind and strength. It is the whole being concentrating on the honour of God and His glory. The context here has a bearing on Jesus' answer. 'Swear by his name' means to perform the oath and keep your promise, to have a full commitment, to be totally dedicated in service and faith, for there will be a reward of glory at the end.

In verse 14 there is the prohibition on idolatry. Jesus used this passage to avoid the sin of self-indulgence; in this instance the worship of self, with the pride of human nature exerting itself at the expense of the honour of God.

In verse 15 we are reminded that God is a "jealous" God. This means being careful about His holy name, His honour, and His unique position in the vast universe. He is Creator of all and any opposition which seeks to rival or displace Him from His true and merited position is rebellion and disobedience.

All this was at stake with this third temptation. God's rightful position as the Lord of the Universe, His reigning supreme in the heart and mind and the life of His Son without any rivals or challengers, was under attack.

This is implicit in the doctrine of the One God. All human life and especially His Son's life, is to be lived with this in mind. Any deviation is sin: it is missing the mark. Another god, another interest, whatever or whoever it is, is covetousness; and covetousness is idolatry, rebellion and sin, coming short of the glory of God.

Conclusions

> Jesus was fighting a hard personal battle within himself, so the victory had to be won within.

The apparent conversation between Jesus and the devil is the thinking of the flesh; this thinking aloud is Jesus' own thoughts.
The arguments put by the *diabolos* were false, by wresting the scriptures and misrepresenting God.
This encounter demonstrates the invidious nature we bear, for it so easily deceives, and provides false security only as transient things are offered.
Jesus knew by heart these Deuteronomy passages – they were a full part of his life.
Jesus knew the experiences of the Children of Israel were his personal challenge.
The foundation clause is Deuteronomy 6:4: "The LORD our God is one LORD". All else flows from this concept – service, single-mindedness, denial of self, unity with the Father.
Jesus made the teaching and message of Deuteronomy a daily living experience.
Having endured the worst and most devious the tempter could challenge him with, he now knew he had been 'humbled, and proved, and what was in his heart'.
He had been tested about his personal needs.
He had been tempted to involve God and the angels in foolish things.
He had been tried in the assertion of self and its exaltation by putting God out of his life.
We have learned from the example of Jesus that "not my will, but thine be done" is a painful and long process.

> Jesus "learned obedience by the things which
> he suffered" and this is the only way to overcome
> temptation.

Although I have taken five chapters to deal with
these three temptations, I believe that Jesus would
have dealt immediately with them 'in a moment of
time'. His recall of scripture and his marshalling of
its teaching and authority were masterly. These three
temptations are typical of what is in the world through
lust, but they were not isolated events in his life.

The account of the temptations in Luke ends with the
words: "When the devil had ended all the temptation,
he departed from him for a season" (Luke 4:13). For the
moment Jesus was triumphant, but the trials would
come back again and again, and with greater force as
the ministry progressed, as he steadfastly set his face
to the cross.

11

THE DEVIL DEPARTED FOR A SEASON

L UKE 4:13 informs us that the devil and therefore temptation only departed from Jesus for a season. How long he had relief from this diabolical force we do not know. But it would be back, with a vengeance.

Enduring suffering

The Gospels and the letters, but especially Hebrews and the Psalms, tell us particularly of the ongoing battle in which the Lord Jesus was engaged during his three-and-a-half-year ministry. It would appear that the temptations came back with more intensity as the ministry developed, so much so that in the Garden of Gethsemane "his sweat was as it were great drops of blood falling down to the ground". This is not to say that the temptations at the beginning of the ministry were easily overcome, for as we have seen, when we have entered into his feelings and realised the forces at work, they were not. The Gospels clearly indicate the struggle that he had in order to remain in control of his fleshly tendencies. Jesus practised what he taught about temptation and its overcoming. He introduced these lessons into the lives and the thinking of his closest followers, so getting them to understand and learn what it meant and what it would cost to be victorious over temptation.

We now explore the Lord's experiences of other similar temptations in his life when the devil returned after its season away. We are familiar with the words of Hebrews 4, that he "was in all points tempted like as we are, yet without sin" (verse 15), and how his suffering and victory overflows into our lives as Hebrews 2 explains:

"For in that he himself hath suffered being tempted, he is able to succour them that are tempted."

(verse 18)

Earlier in Hebrews 2 we are instructed that Jesus, because "he also himself likewise took part of the same" flesh and blood as "the children" (i.e., those he came to save), he experienced the same sensations and the same potential weaknesses. He "suffered" when being tempted in order to triumph over the adversary. The language the apostle uses to describe the agonising is significant. The Greek for "suffered" is *pascho*. We are reminded of the paschal lamb, and the word means 'to experience a sensation (usually painful); to feel, passion, suffer'. The suffering he endured was real. For Jesus this was mental agonising in the extreme. The painful provocation and penetrating probing by 'the devil', felt as the adversarial force during his temptations, certainly needed to be vigorously, consciously, deliberately and continuously repulsed. There was a strong inducement to evil presented to his mind, where it became a trial of virtue and character. He was subjected to this, in a more severe form than was ever presented to others. He was powerfully challenged in his attachment to God.

The three temptations at the beginning of his ministry occurring immediately after his baptism, were representative of what the Apostle John called "the lust of the flesh, and the lust of the eyes, and the pride of life". All the subsequent temptations in Jesus' life fell into one or other of these three categories. In connection with these we shall deal briefly with the mind of the serpent, some other aspects of the wilderness temptation experiences, and those times when all the three kinds of temptation came as one combined event.

The mind of the serpent

It was the enemies of Jesus who adopted the mind and thinking of the serpent in their confrontations with him, especially as the ministry drew to a climax and they closed in on him to spring their ill-conceived trap. The Gospels pick up the language of Eden and the serpent when they describe the manoeuvrings of the Jewish leaders taking shape. The serpent represents the mind and thinking of the flesh and all that opposes the spirit and the purposeful will of God and His Son. We recall the role of the serpent in the downfall of Adam and Eve and the plausibility of its argument; apparently how easily Adam and Eve were overcome, even though they lived in the best of circumstances and had the best of teachers. We recall that their social lives were satisfied by angelic contact, and were at that stage untroubled by sin or the knowledge of good and evil. In remembering all this, we begin to learn just how subtle and devious the serpent was. The serpent clearly thought it had nothing to lose, whereas Adam and Eve had everything to lose, although they chose not to appreciate the full import of the commandment of God, or their fellowship with Him. The serpent in Genesis 3 is described as "more subtle than any beast of the field". We must always bear in mind that the Lord God through the angels had created the beast, presumably to be the means of putting Adam and Eve to the test.

The word "subtle" (Hebrew, *arum*) conveys the idea of cunning (in a bad sense), crafty, prudent. These were the traits or characteristics revealed by the Jewish enemies of Jesus as they harassed him in the ministry and then engineered his arrest, trials and death. They were snakes in the grass with cunning, craft and subtleties. The chief priests, and the scribes, and the elders of the people together with Caiaphas the High Priest, "consulted that they might take Jesus by subtlety, and kill him. But they said, Not on the feast day, lest there be an uproar among the people" (Matthew 26:4,5).

The Sanhedrin consulted to take Jesus by subtlety and kill him, and we note their prudence over which day to make their move and arrest him. Mark's record says, "The chief priests and the scribes sought how they might take him by craft, and put him to death" (14:1). Both Matthew and Mark used the same Greek word (*dolos*) for subtlety and craft, and this carries a meaning of 'trickery, supplying a bait to catch the prey; being wily, deceitful, crafty and demonstrating guile'. It is a word which describes the worst of characters and the worst of intentions. Such were the Jewish leaders. How reminiscent of the serpent!

"And when they had platted a crown of thorns, they put it upon his head, and a reed in his right hand: and they bowed the knee before him, and mocked him, saying, Hail, King of the Jews! And they spit upon him, and took the reed, and smote him on the head." (Matthew 27:29,30)

As part of the fallout of the illegal trials and the unlawful condemnation of Jesus, the soldiers plaited a crown of thorns and thrust it (put it on in a hostile manner) on to his head, and then proceeded to beat him about the head with the reed. To beat means 'to thump', that is to cudgel or to pummel with a stick or a baton with repeated blows. This would physically hurt, but also humiliate and offend the conscience of this innocent man. So Jesus' head was bruised and abused, and just momentarily, the serpent was crushing the head of the seed of the woman. And for the same amount of time, the eternal future hung in the balance. The thorns were also there, part of the aftermath of the fall of Adam and Eve: "The reproaches of them that reproached thee fell on me." (Romans 15:3).

Jesus said of Judas Iscariot that "he ... hath lifted up his heel against me" (John 13:18). It is a clear reference to Genesis 3:15 and the attempt made by the serpent to undermine the divine harmony and purpose of the Garden of Eden. Judas Iscariot manifested serpent behaviour, as he pursued his diabolical betrayal in an attempt to turn Jesus from his sacrificial course and instead rebel against God. But there is also in these words of Jesus an allusion to Jeremiah 17:9. We discovered earlier that the description "deceitful" about the human heart which is desperately wicked, comes from a root word meaning 'to seize by the heel', and we observed then how the heart is related to the serpent and its wicked attitude. So Jesus was describing Judas Iscariot as having serpentine characteristics.

I refer to these things to illustrate the nature of the evil perpetrated against Jesus. Whether it was in secret meetings or revealed in physical violence, all conspired to form part of the temptations that Jesus had to confront and wrestle with. He could so easily have resisted or escaped. He could have worked a miracle or exercised some part of his unlimited powers to resist the evil, especially as the physical violence would really hurt. The temptation to do this must have been present in his heart: to avoid what was being planned against him, or done to him – as it is in our hearts. But had he done so and yielded to his natural inclinations and succumbed to the temptation to escape the situation, that would have frustrated the whole of God's redemptive purpose.

There is a helpful article by Brother Dudley Fifield in *Glimpses of Glory* entitled, "Two temptations".[1] The article compares and contrasts the temptations of Adam and Eve in the Garden of Eden with those of Jesus in the wilderness and his ministry. The intention of the serpent in the testing of Adam and Eve was to set God's law and word aside by slandering God, and getting the first pair to agree with its false accusations. The serpent succeeded. In connection with Jesus' temptations in the wilderness, it was the choice presented by the tempter; the question then was, 'crown or cross – which was to be first?' The response was governed by the answer to another fundamental question, 'Are you sure you can trust God to do as He says, especially in the instruction of the angels to protect you and the promise of resurrection from the dead?' This was a serious charge. The very word of God was being challenged. But Jesus triumphed gloriously in demonstrating his unshakable trust in what was written regardless of the doubts which were voiced by the adversary.

---

1 Originally published in *The Christadelphian*, November 2005, Special Study section, page 419. Reprinted in *Glimpses of Glory,* 2012, page 76.

Reminders of his wilderness experiences

It is useful to see how Matthew recorded the reminders of the wilderness temptations. Four illustrations will suffice. The first is a conversation between Jesus and an earnest scribe:

"And a certain scribe came, and said unto him, Master, I will follow thee whithersoever thou goest. And Jesus saith unto him, The foxes have holes, and the birds of the air have nests; but the Son of man hath not where to lay his head. And another of his disciples said unto him, Lord, suffer me first to go and bury my father. But Jesus said unto him, Follow me; and let the dead bury their dead."

(Matthew 8:19-22)

Superficially this passage seems to have little to do with temptation as Jesus is teaching the scribes and others about commitment and discipleship. But that is just the point! This is reminiscent of Jesus' own attitude when he faced his wilderness temptations. He had in effect said to his Father, 'I will follow you wheresoever you go or lead me'. Jesus himself had no bed to sleep on and on occasions would need to find a cave or a ledge on the hillside. There would have been foxes and birds, wild and other animals. Mark had written, "He was with the wild beasts". Further, there is the excuse made by the scribe, 'let me first', when he saw the difficulties of the calling and hardships resulting from his possible commitment. Jesus' response doesn't give any quarter for compromise. He did not compromise when in the wilderness.

In the parallel account in Luke 9:62, Jesus ended this conversation by saying, "No man, having put his hand to the plough, and looking back, is fit for the kingdom of God". That was a measure of his own commitment and determination to follow the path his Father had chosen for him. Jesus then, preached and taught what he himself had practised during the forty-day wilderness sojourn. He was single-minded, focused and forward looking, and had the realisation that what God had started would be finished. This teaching was about the quality of his own life as well as the disciples' lives and the honouring of vows made; and for himself the fulfilment of the task given to him, even the redemption of the world.

The second illustration is a confrontation with the Pharisees:

"But when the Pharisees heard it, they said, This fellow doth not cast out devils, but by Beelzebub the prince of the devils. And Jesus knew their thoughts, and said unto them, Every kingdom divided against itself is brought to desolation; and every city or house divided against itself shall not stand ... But if I cast out devils by the Spirit of God, then the kingdom of God is come unto you. Or else how can one enter into a strong man's house, and spoil his goods, except he first bind the strong man? and then he will spoil his house."   (Matthew 12:24,25,28,29)

We know the story and how Jesus defeated the illogical argument of the Pharisees. Jesus knew from his time in the wilderness that if he yielded to the pressure of temptation and turned in on himself, allowing the devil power to trample around the house of his mind, which was a dwelling place for God, and undermine his resolve, his house would have been destroyed. He knew that strength of purpose and co-operation with the Father's will was necessary to avoid his downfall and collapse. So this reply to the Pharisees was based on his own actual wilderness experience because he knew it worked! He had been triumphant in his personal warfare because he practised a principle set by his Father which was revealed in the creative acts, his Father's eternal nature and his Holy name. It was harmony and unity fused together by love.

Anything different would have been a recipe for disaster, especially when confronting an enemy as subtle and as powerful as his adversary. So Jesus in his healing miracles confronted 'the demons' in their own house, that is, in the minds and bodies of the sick persons, and overcame them by his power which was much stronger. The Spirit of God was part of the evidence that the kingdom of God was among the people. In the same way in the wilderness, Jesus applied the testimony and wisdom of the Spirit of God, revealed in the mind and the word of God, to his own temptation 'demons' and defeated them utterly.

The next illustration of reminders of the wilderness temptations is found in a parable:

"When the unclean spirit is gone out of a man, he walketh through dry places, seeking rest, and findeth none. Then he saith, I will return into my house from whence I came out; and when he is come, he findeth it empty, swept, and garnished. Then goeth he, and taketh with himself seven other spirits more wicked than himself, and they enter in and dwell there: and the last state of that man is worse than the first."

(Matthew 12:43-45)

The key to this illustration is at end of verse 44, "he findeth it empty, swept, and garnished". The unhelpful thought or distraction had been successfully dealt with and ejected from the mind, but nothing had been done to fill the void, leaving it exposed and "empty, swept, and garnished". A blank canvas is a very inviting place for other thoughts and distractions to find a home and prosper. Might this have been Jesus' wilderness experience? Rejecting one distracting temptation is not done to clear the ground ready for others to enter. He was successful because his mind was full of appropriate and helpful scriptures and godly thoughts, which left no room for negative thinking. Would this be the situation all the time? The determination and perseverance would be there ready to engage in a warfare to the death which was yet to present itself. That warfare would be continuous. The question was, would he always be ready given the unknowns in frequency, circumstances and intensity? The answer from one viewpoint is Yes; but from another is perhaps a cautious No, especially as we are trying to understand the challenges and

129

wrestling in the mind of Jesus and how he would have tackled these big questions.

The answer is Yes, because he always successfully resisted temptation and never left his heart and mind "empty, swept, and garnished". But the answer could have been a possible No, because he was tempted in all points like as we are, and his senses would have been constantly picking up on other distracting things. The fact remains, however, that he was totally successful in resisting all temptation, and any exploration into the possibility of failure or compromise is quite academic and unprofitable. But the point we are attempting to understand is how he evaluated and grappled with each extraneous and unwelcome thought and overcame them, given that he shared the same nature as ourselves.

These incidents demonstrate that temptation returned to the life of Jesus and that it wasn't confined to the first forty days of his public life. The lesson for us is that if nothing is done to maintain our strength of mind, after our single victory overcoming a temptation or whatever weaknesses we are cursed with, then it will return, almost in overwhelming proportions, with "seven other spirits more wicked than [itself]".

The last illustration of wilderness temptation reminders is another clash with the religious leaders and their attitude to the things of God:

"Woe unto you, scribes and Pharisees, hypocrites! for ye make clean the outside of the cup and of the platter, but within they are full of extortion and excess. Thou blind Pharisee, cleanse first that which is within the cup and platter, that the outside of them may be clean also. Woe unto you, scribes and Pharisees, hypocrites! for ye are like unto whited sepulchres, which indeed appear beautiful outward, but are within full of dead men's bones, and of all uncleanness. Even so ye also outwardly appear righteous unto men, but within ye are full of hypocrisy and iniquity ... Ye serpents, ye generation

of vipers, how can ye escape the damnation of hell?"
(Matthew 23:25-28,33)

This is how some temptations appear: outwardly
respectable and honourable, but inwardly devilish
and corrupting. This is how it was for Jesus in the
wilderness as the three temptations came before him.
There was in all the temptations a degree of truth,
which superficially gave them some credibility. 'Turn
the stones into bread'. He was hungry after forty days,
and hunger was a God-given sensation so that bread
can be eaten to prevent malnutrition, and Jesus had
enough power to provide a feast. What was wrong with
making just one loaf? 'Jump from the temple pinnacle
and the angels will catch you'. True, and the prophet
had said so with authority. 'Angels won't let you down,
for you are the beloved Son of God'. No, they wouldn't
fail and he *was* the Son of God. 'Take the kingdoms of
the world; they're yours by promise and inheritance,
every one of them'. They were and again the prophets
had said so. It was true. It was all his by right. Jesus
saw the dangers and by his knowledge of the scriptures
and understanding of the will of God, produced the
right answers. The three temptations were defeated.

It is the same in Matthew 23, when Jesus used three
very powerful cameos in his reproving of the scribes and
Pharisees, as the following table demonstrates:

Outward appearance	The reality within	Result and lesson
Washed the outside of their cups and plates – very good religionists.	Extortion and excess.	Clean the inside first then the outside will be clean.
Decorated the exteriors of graves – very beautiful.	Full of dead men's bones and corruption.	Hypocrisy and iniquity will remain if no repentance.

Built graves for others and furnished them – very commendable.	The graves were those of God's prophets and His righteous people.	These were the sons of those who had killed the prophets – self-deluding unbelief.

Underneath all the outward appearance of beauty and commendable labour in building and fulfilling their own law, lay some distasteful and horrible messes. It was hypocrisy. Fundamentally their motivation was wrong, and so what was seen as their religion was of no value. Is it just possible that this threefold illustration is telling us that, because Jesus knew what was in the hearts of men generally and in the Scribes and Pharisees particularly, it could have been his own experience due to his nature? Could the dangers, which lurked in the hearts of his implacable enemies and revealed by this confrontation, be replicated in himself? Could what appears respectable on the outside be tainted on the inside? This view would be supported by Jeremiah 17:9 and similar passages. It is certainly true of our hearts and minds, and that however hard we try there will always be parts of us which are defective, deviant or deceitful. That's because we are what we are, imperfect creatures of the flesh. And this includes all of us with no exceptions. It is also true to some limited extent of Jesus, because "he also himself likewise took part of the same" flesh and blood.

Three temptations in one

There were some occasions in the life of Jesus when all the three kinds of temptation conspired together as one event; when the full force of the power of sin in the form of "the lust of the flesh, and the lust of the eyes, and the pride of life" all came at once, so testing the Lord Jesus to his limits of faith and endurance. But the circumstances of the events were subtle. We shall look at two which happened in the last week of his mortal life. The first concerns the triumphal entry into Jerusalem a week before the crucifixion.

"And they brought [the colt] to Jesus: and they cast their garments upon the colt, and they set Jesus thereon. And as he went, they spread their clothes in the way. And when he was come nigh, even now at the descent of the mount of Olives, the whole multitude of the disciples began to rejoice and praise God with a loud voice for all the mighty works that they had seen; saying, Blessed be the King that cometh in the name of the Lord: peace in heaven, and glory in the highest. And some of the Pharisees from among the multitude said unto him, Master, rebuke thy disciples. And he answered and said unto them, I tell you that, if these should hold their peace, the stones would immediately cry out." (Luke 19:35-40)
The scene was happy, joyful and peaceful, until the unwanted interruption by the Pharisees. Jesus was riding the ass, going from the Mount of Olives into Jerusalem, with a saddle of soft clothes, and the path decorated with palm leaves. This was a day to remember. Jesus was proclaimed by the people as the King coming "in the name of the LORD", quoting Psalm 118:26, praised for his "mighty works". Jesus chided the Pharisees with the words, "The stones would immediately cry out", if he was denied. With only five or six days to the cross, Jesus was publicly acknowledged as the King of the Jews for the first time in his ministry, and received royally into his capital. It's as if the kingdom could come at any time!

Amongst all this excitement over the King, there is the recognition of his "mighty works". He is being received because of what they had seen and what he could do. These miracles, wonders and signs had been spectacular, like commanding a few loaves into many to feed the crowd twice, as would be the leap from the pinnacle of the temple had it taken place. Jesus would be able to see the stones of the temple and its pinnacles as he approached Jerusalem from Olivet, descending down

133

into and up from the Kidron Valley. Would the memory and the possibility of the second temptation return? The people's acknowledgement was good; otherwise the very stones would add their voice to the testimony that he was the King with mighty works, which gave credence to his claims and preaching. Stones could have been called upon to answer a need some three-and-a-half years earlier: 'change these stones into bread'. They could be now if Jesus was so minded.

Here are subtle references to all the three temptations and what they represented: the lust of the flesh, the lust of the eyes and the pride of life – human need, spectacular mighty works, proclaimed as the King and worshipped by the people. Stones into bread, the pinnacle of the temple, the kingdom – it was all here waiting, again. Had Jesus so desired he could have taken advantage of this moment and established for himself an unassailable position of power and authority – but only for a short period. The temptations this time were prompted by the adulations of the people, but being "drawn away of his own lust" was denied and great self-control was exercised, for he had a message for Jerusalem. His hour was not yet come.

The second event from the last week is very personal to Jesus:

"Then saith he unto them, My soul is exceeding sorrowful, even unto death: tarry ye here, and watch with me. And he went a little further, and fell on his face, and prayed, saying, O my Father, if it be possible, let this cup pass from me: nevertheless not as I will, but as thou wilt. And he cometh unto the disciples, and findeth them asleep, and saith unto Peter, What, could ye not watch with me one hour? Watch and pray, that ye enter not into temptation: the spirit indeed is willing, but the flesh is weak. He went away again the second time, and prayed, saying, O my Father, if this cup may not pass away from me, except I drink it, thy will be done. And he came and found them asleep again: for their eyes were heavy.

134

And he left them, and went away again, and prayed the third time, saying the same words."

(Matthew 26:38-44)

As we meditate on this event in the Garden of Gethsemane we begin to understand dimly the crisis of conscience Jesus was having. Is he trying to avoid the cross and have his Father find another way? Is he praying to find the strength to accept the cross? There is a conflict, an agony. He was 'grieved all around, intensely sad'. The words of verse 38, "exceeding sorrowful" are very strong and weighty. It all came from within; he was deeply troubled.

The Psalms were being fulfilled in their detail, particularly Psalm 22:10-16. There were many others which were coming to life at this moment of death, for example, Psalms 18:4,5; 38:1-4,8-12; 42:7; 55:4,5; 69:1-3; 88:3,4; 116:3.

"Let this cup pass from me ... thy will be done". This oscillation of his intense feelings, these moments of apparent unwillingness prompted by human weakness and fearfulness, the surge of strength to overcome the doubts and fears, resulted in eventual victory. The cup would not pass from him, for "man doth not live by bread only, but by every word that proceedeth out of the mouth of the LORD doth man live". So "thy will be done". The cup would be drunk. His Father, having spoken the word, could not be persuaded to let the cup pass. But Jesus would not 'tempt the Lord his God' and put Him to the test. Had the cup passed from him in answer to his prayer, and had he not drunk it as he had prayed, the flesh would have triumphed and self would not have been denied. Sin would have been committed and become the master, and salvation impossible. God would have been challenged and His word and will no longer supreme. Yet he would 'worship the Lord [his] God, and serve him only'. The three temptations of the wilderness reappeared at this time of crisis. The answers Jesus gave in the first lonely place were repeated again in this lonely place.

135

12

IN THE DAY OF TEMPTATION

W E consider now the temptation to turn stones into bread, and how it came back repeatedly to test the resolve of the Lord Jesus.

This temptation was not just about bread or food or the need to satisfy a basic natural human condition, it was also about the lust of the flesh and its cravings in all its myriad forms. Just as a leap from a pinnacle of the temple was about letting the angels protect him, as well as the pride of life coupled with personal ambition and endeavour; or taking the kingdoms of the world was not just about kingship, it also embraced the lust of the eyes and the desire to have power and influence over others.

The temptation to turn the stones into bread is about getting or having material benefits, self-preservation, and having human needs of all kinds fulfilled. As all these things are temporal, they can be referred to as 'bread'. Joshua and Caleb described the indigenous inhabitants of Canaan in the same way when they made their spy-report to the people:

"... neither fear ye the people of the land; for they are bread for us."   (Numbers 14:9)

In other words, 'we regard them as next to nothing, inconsequential and transient', they said, with their confidence in the Lord God.

"No time to eat"

It is helpful to consider four passages from Mark's Gospel which illustrate the busyness of the ministry and the occasional lack of opportunity to satisfy their hunger. Sometimes, there was no time to eat because of their crowded schedule.

"And the multitude cometh together again, so that they could not so much as eat bread." (Mark 3:20)

"And he said unto them, Come ye yourselves apart into a desert place, and rest a while: for there were many coming and going, and they had no leisure so much as to eat." (6:31)

"In those days the multitude being very great, and having nothing to eat, Jesus called his disciples unto him, and saith unto them, I have compassion on the multitude, because they have now been with me three days, and have nothing to eat." (8:1,2)

"And on the morrow, when they were come from Bethany, he was hungry." (11:12)

Peter's eyewitness accounts in Mark perhaps describe the poverty of the immediate twelve, but also demonstrate the emphasis which was placed on the more important spiritual work and lessons implicit in the Gospel. The need to eat was not a top priority.

Matthew also has a sequence of references which relate to bread, hunger and eating. These are equally instructive as the following three passages show:

"At that time Jesus went on the sabbath day through the corn; and his disciples were an hungred, and began to pluck the ears of corn, and to eat. But when the Pharisees saw it, they said unto him, Behold, thy disciples do that which is not lawful to do upon the sabbath day." (Matthew 12:1,2)

The disciples were hungry and picked the ears of corn partially to satiate that hunger. Jesus did not provide miraculously for either their or his own needs, despite the necessity or his ability. This event took place on a sabbath, and explanations about the true meaning of the sabbath day engaged their attention, rather than stating the obvious about their hunger. Matthew next gives an account of the feeding of the five thousand (14:14-22) on the basis of compassion; followed by the feeding of the four thousand on the same grounds (15:32-39). Then in chapter 16 he records an incident about the misunderstanding the disciples had over

137

Jesus' comments relating to the attitude of the Jewish leaders. The quotations from Matthew 15 and 16 follow:

"Then Jesus called his disciples unto him, and said, I have compassion on the multitude, because they continue with me now three days, and have nothing to eat: and I will not send them away fasting, lest they faint in the way." (15:32)

"And when his disciples were come to the other side, they had forgotten to take bread. Then Jesus said unto them, Take heed and beware of the leaven of the Pharisees and of the Sadducees. And they reasoned among themselves, saying, It is because we have taken no bread. Which when Jesus perceived, he said unto them, O ye of little faith, why reason ye among yourselves, because ye have brought no bread?" (16:5-8)

Again the twelve have no food and are worried as Jesus chided them for their lack of understanding and faith. At this point, according to Mark 8:17,18, Jesus made an oblique reference to Isaiah:

"Hear ye indeed, but understand not; and see ye indeed, but perceive not. Make the heart of this people fat, and make their ears heavy, and shut their eyes; lest they see with their eyes, and hear with their ears, and understand with their heart, and convert, and be healed." (6:9,10)

The purpose of this was to remind the disciples that they should not close their heart, eyes or ears to his ability and willingness to provide all things for them, especially their daily bread. The Isaiah passage is about the wilful refusal to hear and see the wonderful works of God, and the folly of concentrating on things that would pass away due to their corrupt and temporary nature. The twelve were thinking about bread at the mundane level, instead of lifting their hearts and opening their eyes, ears and understanding to what Jesus had done with five loaves and two fish for five thousand, and seven loaves and a few fish for four thousand. What would he not do for the twelve whom he loved? He would do whatever was necessary, but in due time and at the right time when the more important duties were completed.

I have referred to these two events to show, on the one hand, that Jesus did not provide automatically for the twelve even though they were hungry; but on the other hand, because of reasons of compassion he miraculously fed over nine thousand hungry people. There is no inconsistency or conflict, and it does not mean he lacked compassion for the disciples.

Earlier we saw that Jesus introduced the disciples to the lesson that "man doth not live by bread only, but by every word that proceedeth out of the mouth of the LORD doth man live". These two incidents illustrate that teaching. Jesus resisted the temptation to produce bread for the twelve, including himself because (1) there were more pressing reasons why he should not do so, and (2) he needed the disciples to learn God's principles for true living, and the priorities which should motivate and guide their lives.

Feeding the people

Mark's record of the feeding of the five thousand tells us that it could well have brought before Jesus the first temptation of 'stones into bread':

> "And he said unto them, Come ye yourselves apart into a desert place, and rest a while: for there were many coming and going, and they had no leisure so much as to eat. And they departed into a desert place by ship privately. And the people saw them departing, and many knew him, and ran afoot thither out of all cities, and out-went them, and came together unto him. And Jesus, when he came out, saw much people, and was moved with compassion toward them, because they were as sheep not having a shepherd: and he began to teach them many things. And when the day was now far spent, his disciples came unto him, and said, This is a desert place, and now the time is far passed: send them away, that they may go into the country round about, and into the villages,

and buy themselves bread: for they have nothing to eat. He answered and said unto them, Give ye them to eat." (Mark 6:31-37)

The setting for this miracle is recorded three times: "a desert place" – the same kind of place as the wilderness temptations. Although Jesus had taken the twelve into the desert, "to rest a while", the day had been anything but a time of rest, and they had spent it "teaching many things". The people were as "sheep not having a shepherd", another wilderness allusion. They were lost and needed to be found, as wanderers who needed direction in their lives. There was a discussion at the end of the day about an evening meal. 'Let the people go and buy bread from the village shops', was one solution. No! said Jesus, and the twelve were invited to feed them, apparently with nothing!

This is not a temptation in the same way as it was presented in the wilderness, but nevertheless a situation had arisen which must have reminded Jesus about the command to "turn these stones into bread", and the ease with which this task could be accomplished for the benefit of all. He was in a desert place, with rocks and stones strewn all over the ground, the hunger of the people was obvious and there was an urgent need to satisfy them. He asked the disciples to get what the people had. Not that they could be satisfied with five loaves and two fish humanly speaking, but this offering when blended with compassion and his prayer of thanksgiving coupled to the blessing from heaven, would feed five thousand with fragments over. He would work with what the people had and turn it into a feast for their benefit. Jesus resisted the temptation to turn stones into bread for himself in the wilderness, but then used that same power to produce food for the people out of their own resources.

Mark also provides an account of the feeding of the four thousand:

"I have compassion on the multitude, because they have now been with me three days, and have nothing

140

to eat: and if I send them away fasting to their own houses, they will faint by the way: for divers of them came from far. And his disciples answered him, From whence can a man satisfy these men with bread here in the wilderness? And he asked them, How many loaves have ye? And they said, Seven." (Mark 8:2-5) We are brought face to face with the predicament of the four thousand, as three days away from home and the comforts it provided, left them without the means to feed themselves. Jesus was putting the disciples to the test to see what response they could offer to satisfy the multitude's needs. Verse 4 is an expression of their doubt, but the passage also tells us about Jesus' compassion to provide and his ability to perform mighty works. The disciples' answer revealed their incredulity that such a multitude could be adequately fed and satisfied in a wilderness. The disciples had not yet learned the lesson of the five thousand, the power of their Lord, or yet of his compassion. Their question, their doubt, is very close to the thrust of Psalm 78 as these few verses show:

"And they sinned yet more against him by provoking the most High in the wilderness. And they tempted God in their heart by asking meat for their lust. Yea, they spoke against God; they said, Can God furnish a table in the wilderness? Behold, he smote the rock, that the waters gushed out, and the streams overflowed; can he give bread also? can he provide flesh for his people?" (Psalm 78:17-20)

This psalm is about the rebelliousness of the Children of Israel, which was manifest from the time of their exodus from Egypt to the reign of King David, despite the Lord God acting generously and wondrously for them. It tells of their unbelief that the Lord could provide for and satisfy human needs in barren places, and had done so marvellously and dramatically all that time. The people had about a thousand years of history behind them, which spoke eloquently of God's involvement in their nation, its survival and salvation.

141

There was blindness, and a lack of understanding; taking 'the commonplace' for granted which got in the way of a full appreciation of the wonderful works of God. There is also in this record a reference to the Wilderness of Sin, to Massah and Meribah, places where complaints were made about the lack of bread and water. A sample of the daily manna was gathered into a pot and laid up before the Testimony to be kept (see Exodus 16:33,34), as a permanent reminder for succeeding generations of God's care and His miraculous provision. There was considerable evidence that God could "furnish a table in the wilderness".

Massah (Exodus 17:1-7) as we have already seen, was the place at which spiritual drink came out of the spiritual rock which followed them, and that rock was Christ (1 Corinthians 10:4). This is a significant reference, for in answering the second temptation to leap from the pinnacle of the temple, Jesus had said, "Thou shalt not tempt the Lord thy God", and the passage he quoted came from Deuteronomy (6:16) concluding with, "as ye tempted him in Massah".

The twelve had unwittingly fallen into the same trap as unfaithful Israel, who considered that with little or no resources and in a barren place, not much could be done. But they had forgotten what can be done, and had failed to see the connection between Christ's purpose and his concerns for the ordinary people and their needs. With seven loaves and a few fish, the giving of thanks, the added blessing from heaven, four thousand were satisfied. Again Jesus had used the power of the Spirit in favour of the many people in the desert, to supply the same need that he had experienced in the wilderness. But then such use for himself was denied, "for man shall not live by bread alone".

Problems at Bethany – "that good part"

Luke describes a homely picture where tensions arose over domestic duties, and the apparent inequality of the workload. It is a familiar scene:

"Now it came to pass, as they went, that he entered into a certain village: and a certain woman named Martha received him into her house. And she had a sister called Mary, which also sat at Jesus' feet, and heard his word. But Martha was cumbered about much serving, and came to him, and said, Lord, dost thou not care that my sister hath left me to serve alone? bid her therefore that she help me. And Jesus answered and said unto her, Martha, Martha, thou art careful and troubled about many things: but one thing is needful: and Mary hath chosen that good part, which shall not be taken away from her."

(Luke 10:38-42)

This passage is connected to the temptation to turn stones into bread, in view of Martha being "cumbered about much serving", and demanding that Jesus tell Mary to help her. Jesus could so easily have provided a meal for the large party, so relieving Martha of her anxieties and her chiding; then she too could have sat at Jesus' feet and heard his word. Yet, Jesus was pressing home on his closest followers, and especially on Martha at this time, the spiritual lesson he had confirmed in the wilderness that "man doth not live by bread only". Mary seems to have understood this, at least on this occasion, because Martha like ourselves needed reminding and was duly instructed, that "one thing is needful: and Mary hath chosen that good part". It is possible that Mary needed and wanted to learn to live "by every word that proceeded out of the mouth of the Lord" and make up for lost opportunities in her life, especially if she was "Mary called Magdalene, out of whom went seven devils". This implies an unprofitable life for whatever reason. Of course, if we all sat at the feet of Jesus and heard his word all the time, nothing would get done, either domestically or in ecclesial life. There is a time to sit and a time to serve, "a time to cast away stones, and a time to gather stones together" (Ecclesiastes 3:5). We have to learn where the balance is. Even Jesus expected the twelve to work and eat, and have enough to spare, and he didn't provide for their

143

needs except on rare occasions, for "every man should eat and drink, and enjoy the good of all his labour, it is the gift of God" (verse 13).

Walking no more with him

John 6 begins with the feeding of the five thousand. In his assessment of the people, as we have already learned from Mark's Gospel, Jesus saw them as "sheep not having a shepherd", abandoned by their so-called spiritual mentors. The people needed support and assistance. Being fed by Jesus could have turned them toward God, had they recognised the authority behind the miracle. But a different reaction resulted:

> "Jesus answered them and said, Verily, verily, I say unto you, Ye seek me, not because ye saw the miracles, but because ye did eat of the loaves, and were filled. Labour not for the meat which perisheth, but for that meat which endureth unto everlasting life, which the Son of man shall give unto you."
>
> (John 6:26,27)

The discourse of John 6 following this miracle of feeding the five thousand, is concerned with "the bread of life" and was structured to teach the people that "man doth not live by bread only, but by every word that proceedeth out of the mouth of the LORD". The people had quickly realised that here was a prophet who could provide for their immediate benefit as well as the good of the nation. They were not ready or prepared to receive his teaching and the next day clamoured for more bread, but got none. John (verse 15) tells us that as a result of this miracle, "Jesus perceived that they would come and take him by force, to make him a king". So kingship and the third temptation was raising its head, hence "he departed again into a mountain himself alone" – no doubt to pray and resist the celebrity being pressed upon him.

It was Jesus' reaction to the crowd who had followed him back to Capernaum that is striking. He knew their needs; they were just as hungry as the day before when he fed them. His compassion for them had not diminished. But he also knew their motives, now clamouring after him for all the wrong reasons: "ye did eat of the loaves, and were filled" (verse 26). They had not perceived that the miracle he worked in producing bread was not an end in itself. It spoke of his Sonship, of his being the Christ their anointed King; in fact, the "prophet that should come into the world" (verse 14). This is why Jesus speaks of eternal things at the expense of the temporal: "Labour not for the meat which perisheth, but for that meat which endureth unto everlasting life" (verse 27). There is a time to eat, as the people had enjoyed the day before, but there is also a time to sit at Jesus' feet and hear his word. When the opportunity is provided it must be taken. But when he spoke to them, they did not listen:

"They said therefore unto him, What sign showest thou then, that we may see, and believe thee? what dost thou work?" (verse 30)

This is incredible! The sign had been shown, five thousand people had seen it, but it had not been believed, or the work itself recognised as an evidence of his divine authority and Sonship. There is no record of Jesus providing bread on this occasion. In fact, this event and the discourse which followed became a watershed in the relationship between the people and Jesus, even between some of his disciples and Jesus; so that "from that time many of his disciples went back, and walked no more with him" (verse 66). The teaching in Deuteronomy 8:1-6 that "man doth not live by bread only, but by every word that proceedeth out of the mouth of the LORD doth man live", and which Jesus applied with such rigour to himself during his wilderness temptations, proved a stumbling block to both disciples and people alike. They had heard and spoken to the greatest Teacher the world had seen, and had the evidence of his authority before them on a daily basis, if only they would recognise it, but still they could not accept the full import of the message. The teaching was too demanding to accept. It meant leaving their comfort zones for a different kind of life. The paradigm shift was just too great.

How much more do we need to learn the same lesson, that we only truly begin to live when we believe and practise "every word that proceedeth out of the mouth of the LORD"!

13

YOU HAVE CONTINUED WITH ME
IN MY TEMPTATIONS

LUKE tells us (22:28) that when Jesus was in the upper room on the last evening of his earthly life, he spoke of his temptations as continuing throughout his ministry and about to climax in the cross. The fact that the temptations were continuous indicates that the cross was not an isolated event in his life separate from all else. The cross was an integral part. It was the climax and the whole purpose of his life. It is why all the temptations came, in order to prepare him and make him strong for the one final test.

As he encouraged the twelve in Luke 22, he was lonely and isolated. In verse 21 there is reference to his betrayal; in verse 24 strife began among the disciples about who was the greatest and most important. The twelve could easily have weakened Jesus' resolve and deflected him off course with this kind of behaviour and attitude, had he not been strong and single-minded in his love for his Father and the great purpose he was poised to fulfil.

But greater pain than the squabbles among the twelve was only hours away: the agony of the Garden of Gethsemane, the arrest, trials both Jewish and Roman, then crucifixion with all its associated horrors, and finally death.

The pinnacle of the temple repeated
The pinnacle of the temple temptation was not just about the promised protection by the angels, as wonderful as that would be. It was also about doing miracles, wonders and signs to impress others; being popular and pursuing popularity for its own sake; doing the spectacular thing to create and enhance a

personal image; in short, a pride of life scenario with self-promotion and ambition for greatness and power. These things needed to be repudiated, if Jesus were to be of a humble and contrite heart, without spot and blemish, prepared as the perfect sacrifice.

His nature, with its inherent but for the most part latent basic weaknesses, would stimulate opportunities for such self-promotion to recur time and again had Jesus allowed it the upper hand. He would be severely tested, tempted and tried in his loyalty to God, and in the acknowledgement of his true human relationship before God, so much so that on one occasion he said, "Why callest thou me good? there is none good but one, that is, God". He certainly felt the pull of the flesh with its deviant ways.

We shall learn by looking at a number of incidents in the Gospels how this temptation to leap from a pinnacle of the temple was repeated, continually plaguing him to the very last. We shall consider the eight cameos listed below, but there are probably others which could fit into this same pattern:

The thrust over the brow of the hill

Jesus threatened with stoning

They seek a sign

Signs by the power of Beelzebub

Show yourself to the world

Gethsemane

Jewish trials

On the cross

The thrust over the brow of the hill

This incident occurred early in the ministry and followed Jesus' revelations and prophesying in the synagogue at Nazareth, when he read from the prophet Isaiah. Luke summarises the reactions of the hearers:

"And all they in the synagogue, when they heard these things, were filled with wrath, and rose up, and thrust him out of the city, and led him unto the brow of the hill whereon their city was built, that they might cast him down headlong. But he passing through the midst of them went his way."

(Luke 4:28-30)

When we compare this description with the language and meaning of Luke 4:9-11, which is the narrative of his wilderness testing, we can easily see there is a recurrence of the pinnacle of the temple temptation. Jesus knew that if he was pushed over the edge of the hill, the angels would bear him up to keep him, lest he dashed his foot against a stone, if he so wished and God so willed. The promise was there. But on this occasion he was not going voluntarily; he was being thrust out from the city by angry people. The word "thrust" (Greek, *ekballo)* is to eject, drive out, expel, send away from. It is a strong active word.

He was thrust out, yet he came to his own as a resident of Nazareth, "and his own received him not" (John 1:11). They "led him unto the brow of the hill", forcibly and with intent to murder him. Jesus was taken reluctantly much against his will. "Led" (Greek, *ago)* is the same word as Luke (4:1) uses in describing Jesus going into the wilderness immediately after his baptism. This means he was led to the brow of the hill at Nazareth in the same way as he "was led by the Spirit into the wilderness" to be tempted.

Mark (1:12) tells us "the Spirit driveth him into the wilderness", at the beginning of all his temptations, and the word "driveth" here is the same word as "thrust out" in the passage from Luke 4:29. It means he was "thrust out" of Nazareth in the same way as "the Spirit driveth him into the wilderness" – with force and involuntarily.

Given the words the Gospel writers use, we can appreciate the force and opposition that was being applied to him, both at the beginning of the wilderness temptations, and also in Nazareth. The implication is that in neither case did he really want to go. Also (verse 29), we note how they intended to "cast him down headlong", which compares with (4:9) "cast

149

thyself down". Again this is another strong word, and frequently denotes 'opposition or intensity', being a description of the hatred and intent of the synagogue worshippers against Jesus.

The text here (verse 29) with the repeated emphasis on "thrust", "led", and "cast him down headlong", is drawing on the earlier events of the wilderness temptations. There was no doubt that the Nazareth scene was a recurrence of the temptation to leap from the pinnacle of the temple and be saved by the angels. How would Jesus deal with it? What did he do?

The answer is given in verse 30, but what does it really mean? There is nothing unusual about the words "passing through", or "midst", meaning among or between them. The picture is of a crowd of angry people rushing to the hilltop with Jesus trapped among them, so he couldn't escape. They were determined to throw him over the edge to kill him, when he passes through them without let or hindrance, and is free. What happened?

Did he use the Holy Spirit power to escape? Were the people temporarily blinded, as in Sodom over the protection of Lot and his family, or like the Syrians of Elisha's day? Or were the people filled with confusion, so they couldn't do what they planned? Did the angels come according to the promise of Psalm 91: "He shall give his angels charge over thee, to keep thee in all thy ways"? More than likely.

The similarity between this event and the wilderness temptation is that Jesus did not and would not leap from the temple pinnacle or the brow of the hill, in order to provoke God and the angels into saving action. Here however, although Jesus was never a victim of circumstance, he was caught in the machinations of devious and aggressive men. But "his hour was not yet come" and it is reasonable to accept that the angels intervened. There is no conflict. "He ... went his way." The emphasis must be on "his way", that is, the way of God, the way of the spirit, the way of obedience;

whereas the synagogue worshippers went back to their way in their house of death.

Jesus threatened with stoning

This event is a repeat of the pinnacle of the temple temptation, but it occurred towards the end of the ministry and within three to six months of the cross:

"Then took they up stones to cast at him; but Jesus hid himself, and went out of the temple, going through the midst of them, and so passed by."

(John 8:59)

The scene is set in Jerusalem. The difference between this incident and the previous one is the intention to stone Jesus. He hid himself to avoid an illegal summary judgement, but also, like before, his time "was not yet come". It also avoided an anticipation of his greater crisis to come, and bringing his adversaries to an early judgement themselves. Jesus was in a hazardous situation. The word "hid" (Greek, *krupto*) means 'to conceal (properly by covering), hide, to keep secret, secretly'. It is the same word which describes Adam and Eve 'hiding themselves' amongst the trees in the Garden of Eden for fear of meeting with the angel of God in Genesis 3:8,10 (LXX). *Krupto* definitely means 'hid himself'.

We cannot suggest for one moment that Jesus ran away and hid behind some large temple pillar playing a desperate game of hide and seek with the Pharisees, Levites and the temple police. It may be possible that Jesus was hidden (although the Greek hardly means this) by the power and intervention of the angels, so that those looking for him couldn't find him. Maybe they had temporary confusion or a form of blindness to prevent them searching him out. Whatever happened, John says that Jesus "hid himself" and could not be discovered, so he "passed by" as he did on the former occasion.

It is worth considering three short passages from the Psalms which are relevant to this pursuing and hiding. The first is a prayer for safety; the second a prayer in the event of vendettas; and the third expresses great confidence that the promised protection would be forthcoming.

"Hear my prayer, O LORD, and let my cry come unto thee. Hide not thy face from me in the day when I am in trouble; incline thine ear unto me: in the day when I call answer me speedily."   (Psalm 102:1,2)

"Hear my voice, O God, in my prayer: preserve my life from fear of the enemy. Hide me from the secret counsel of the wicked; from the insurrection of the workers of iniquity: who whet their tongue like a sword, and bend their bows to shoot their arrows, even bitter words: that they may shoot in secret at the perfect: suddenly do they shoot at him, and fear not."   (Psalm 64:1-4)

"Though an host should encamp against me, my heart shall not fear: though war should rise against me, in this will I be confident ... For in the time of trouble he shall hide me in his pavilion: in the secret of his tabernacle shall he hide me: he shall set me up upon a rock."   (Psalm 27:3,5)

These three short extracts from the Psalms reveal something of the real anxieties experienced by Jesus during these extremely tense and difficult times. They were of course life-threatening situations, and needed to be coped with practically for the sake of his disciples and their divine education, but also balanced by the commitment already made to the Father and the Father's endorsement of the Son at his baptism. So there was a spiritual dimension which had to be accounted for in the solutions which were found to these unfriendly conditions, when "his hour was not yet come".

It would be totally unreasonable to assume that Jesus felt nothing of the normal fears and suspicions as a man when these situations arose. Because "he knew what was in man", he was aware of the evil motives of such a hostile crowd when they forced him in their midst to the top of the hill. So these Psalms are relevant to the immediate problem and teach us how quickly Jesus could focus on the word of God to find his answers.

In voicing these prayers Jesus was expressing his complete confidence in the safety promised by his Father, and his Father's willingness to act according to His righteousness and the ultimate fulfilment of His purpose. "The LORD is my light and my salvation; whom shall I fear?" The Lord Jesus' faith in the word and his hope in the Father's love are the means which lift him up beyond the prevailing threatening circumstances to find his peace and serenity. This was one more occasion when he lived "by every word that proceeded out of the mouth of the LORD" – and there were many during the ministry.

Jesus' safety in "passing through the midst of them" is the answer to his prayer and God sending the angels as promised in Psalm 91. There is no conflict between the angelic work in this instance and Jesus' refusal to invoke the same help in the wilderness temptation. Jesus being hidden is the divine answer to the people taking up stones to throw at him. In this connection, we observe the following sequence:

"Then the Jews took up stones again to stone him."   (John 10:31)

"Therefore they sought again to take him: but he escaped out of their hand."   (verse 39)

"His disciples say unto him, Master, the Jews of late sought to stone thee; and goest thou thither again?"   (11:8)

Each occasion would demand the same kind of intense prayer to escape the violence, "for his hour was not yet come". There was no room for the spectacular. The temptation was rejected and the spirit triumphed.

They seek a sign

Occasionally Jesus was expected to produce a sign to satisfy the curiosity of the nation's religious leaders. He was asked to do a spectacular thing, just for its own sake, with no objective in view, nor anyone who could benefit. There must have been considerable frustration, both on the Lord's part because of the demands they made, and in those who did not get their way to enjoy a possible spectacle.

"The Pharisees also with the Sadducees came, and tempting desired him that he would show them a sign from heaven. He answered and said unto them, When it is evening, ye say, It will be fair weather: for the sky is red. And in the morning, It will be foul weather today: for the sky is red and lowring. O ye hypocrites, ye can discern the face of the sky; but can ye not discern the signs of the times? A wicked and adulterous generation seeks after a sign; and there shall no sign be given unto it, but the sign of the prophet Jonas. And he left them, and departed."

(Matthew 16:1-4)

This scene followed immediately after Jesus had sent away the multitude of four thousand after feeding them, and the disciples had collected up a considerable amount of fragments. He then took a boat and crossed over the Lake of Galilee to Magdala. Mark (8:12) adds what may be construed as the sign of frustration or even great disappointment at their facetious incredulity, "he sighed deeply in his spirit".

The Greek for "sighed deeply" (*ana-stenazo*) is another compound Greek word. In this case one word (*ana*) relates to the 'sighing', meaning 'to be in straits, to sigh, murmur or pray inaudibly with grief or groan'. The other word (*stenazo*) relates to 'deeply', and when used in conjunction with *ana*, means 'with intensity, and repetition'. It is Jesus' inner distress with an external expression.

We could read Mark's phrase as meaning that Jesus prayed with intensity and continuously but inaudibly, so that it sounded like sighing, perhaps in order to overcome any anger, disappointment or frustration welling up within him, and that he felt towards the Pharisees and Sadducees because of their incredulous demands and unbelief.

154

In *The Gospel of the Son of God* by Brother Sargent, another suggestion has been presented:

> "Only Mark records the sigh from the depth of the heart, called forth by human perversity. These barren meetings with the Pharisees not only called for intellectual acumen from Jesus, but they brought emotional strain."[1]

The reason for this is that the Pharisees and scribes had sallied forth, as in an ambush, and "began to argue with him, seeking a sign from heaven", as though to put him to proof, and end the so-called uncertainty they had about Jesus. The demand was specious by those putting it but not willing to be convinced. The perversity of the Pharisees and Sadducees is compounded by the fact that earlier on the very same day, across the other side of the lake, Jesus had just fed four thousand people from seven loaves and a few fish, with seven baskets of fragments over! It is difficult to imagine that news of this extraordinary event had not spread in and around the district as soon as it had happened.

What more did they want as evidence of his Sonship and his being the Christ? There were four thousand witnesses to his authority and power! Jesus told them they would have "no sign but the sign of the prophet Jonah" (Matthew 16:4), indicating his resurrection from the dead after three days. This was the second time this sign had been given to the Pharisees. But this witness was of course post-resurrection! Ironically the Sadducees did not believe in the resurrection; so whatever Jesus did or said on this matter, they would remain in unbelief. As a result there was no spectacular miracle, wonder or sign.

Again, in *The Gospel of the Son of God* (page 110), we read:

> "To grant what they wanted would not only be ineffectual to dispel wilful blindness; he would by their prompting succumb to the temptation he had

---

1 Brother L. G. Sargent, *The Gospel of the Son of God*, 1966, page 110.

rejected in the wilderness of putting God to the proof".

Why? "Thou shalt not tempt the Lord thy God."

Signs by the power of Beelzebub

We consider now the first occasion when Jesus gave the scribes and Pharisees the sign of the prophet Jonah. This is just after he was tempted to perform the spectacular and do a miracle, which was the equivalent of the leap off the pinnacle of the temple.

"Then certain of the scribes and of the Pharisees answered, saying, Master, we would see a sign from thee. But he answered and said unto them, An evil and adulterous generation seeketh after a sign; and there shall no sign be given to it, but the sign of the prophet Jonas; for as Jonas was three days and three nights in the whale's belly; so shall the Son of man be three days and three nights in the heart of the earth." (Matthew 12:38-40)

We should notice the references in this chapter to the Pharisees in verses 2,14,24; "generation of vipers" in verse 34, scribes and Pharisees in verse 38. It was an unpleasant scene in which there was confrontation and opposition, with the authorities seeking to destroy Jesus and condemn him by his words and actions. It would have been challenging, frustrating and tempting. One wonders if they had thought about the words of Isaiah, "... that make a man an offender for a word, and lay a snare for him that reproveth in the gate, and turn aside the just for a thing of nought" (Isaiah 29:21).

As in the example taken earlier from Matthew 16, the demand was for "a sign from thee", in order to satisfy curiosity and seek evidence to take counsel to destroy him. Jesus knew it was devious and he called them a "generation of vipers", serpent-thinking people. The Pharisees had demonstrated this when they attributed the works of Jesus to the power of Beelzebub the adversary. Their cunning in seeking the sign was on the back of his healing work and the grateful acknowledgement by the people that he was the long promised Old Testament Messiah.

"But when the Pharisees heard it, they said, This fellow doth not cast out devils, but by Beelzebub the prince of the devils." (Matthew 12:24)

The Pharisees had heard that the one who was deaf and therefore dumb and also blind, either a man or a woman, was healed of all three disabilities and restored to full health. Here was a wonderful witness and sign with Jesus demonstrating he was the Lord of Life. Even the people recognised his authority and true paternity when they said, "Is not this the Son of David?" What more was needed?

No other sign from heaven would be provided except the sign of the prophet Jonah. There would be a resurrection after three days, but this witness would not be available for some time yet, and would not satisfy the Sadducees in any event. The need to exercise faith was paramount.

Jesus reinforced his superiority and authority as the Son of God over Jonah (verse 41), and Solomon (verse 42). He drew attention to Jonah's preaching because of Nineveh's repentance, and to Solomon's wisdom, because it convinced the Queen of Sheba. Both the Queen and the Ninevites were Gentiles! Additionally, Jonah came back to life when he should have been dead, and Solomon expanded the kingdom of Israel to the largest borders ever enjoyed, and increased the wealth and influence of the nation beyond all expectations. They were the glory days under the king. But Jesus was even greater than both. Jesus was the King of the Jews by right, and the Greater Son of David by holy birth – as Solomon never was. Jesus would come back to life without corruption to live forever.

There was an underlying and powerful teaching involved in: (1) healing miracles and signs; (2) the need for the people to believe him for the very works' sake – the things he had done should have been sufficient for faith; (3) his refusal to succumb to the pressure

157

and temptation to do conjuring tricks to amuse his
unbelieving critics, namely the Pharisees, Sadducees
and scribes; and (4) he would not leap from the pinnacle
of the temple, and perform spectacular stunts to put
God to the proof. His faith did not need that kind of
extravagant evidence.

"Show thyself to the world"

There was an occasion only about six months from the
cross when he was tested to see if he would press home
his popularity with the people. The pressure on him
was unrelenting, but this time it came from his close
but unbelieving family.

"His brethren therefore said unto him, Depart
hence, and go into Judaea, that thy disciples also
may see the works that thou doest. For there is no
man that doeth anything in secret, and he himself
seeks to be known openly. If thou do these things,
show thyself to the world."   (John 7:3,4)

This was subtle. His brethren had another agenda; he
was embarrassing them and they did not believe him,
his claims or his works. What they said was the way of
the flesh, but it contained elements of truth as it usually
does, because "the heart is deceitful above all things,
and desperately sick: who can know it?" When we hear
his brethren speak, it is with serpentine tongues and
with hearts full of guile, for they said, 'Your disciples
in Judaea would like to see your miracles, wonders and
signs'.

No doubt they would; for they might have seen it as
very odd, that a man who needed to be known by a wider
audience because of his saving message, did all his
works in private. But his family did not understand. So
they said, 'Reveal yourself, do your works publicly, seek
your glory and popularity'. They reasoned just like the
serpent of Genesis 3 which spoke in half-truths, made
some false suggestions, had a faulty understanding,
and probed what it thought were possible weaknesses.
His brethren said, 'Be something you're not; be a
stuntman, impress the people'. But it was spoken out

158

of enmity, and not out of love or support. The Psalmist had already anticipated this, "I am become a stranger unto my brethren, and an alien unto my mother's children" (Psalm 69:8). The temptation was denied, for "My time is not yet come" (John 7:6). But it would come in about six months. So there was no spectacular sign, but the temptation was powerful and subtle.

Gethsemane

We move to the events at the end of the ministry in the Garden of Gethsemane, then the Jewish trials, and finally the cross. The second temptation reappears, most emphatically:

> "Then said Jesus unto him, Put up again thy sword into his place: for all they that take the sword shall perish with the sword. Thinkest thou that I cannot now pray to my Father, and he shall presently give me more than twelve legions of angels? But how then shall the scriptures be fulfilled, that thus it must be?" (Matthew 26:52-54)

Peter unwisely wielded the sword in Jesus' defence with catastrophic results for Malchus the High Priest's servant. The temptation which was in danger of reasserting itself was the summoning of the angels, possibly in excess of seventy-two thousand. That would really be spectacular! The key to their coming was "Now I pray to my Father". This would invoke the promise of Psalm 91, "He shall give his angels charge over thee, to keep thee in all thy ways".

He knew his Father would not fail him and he could escape his desperate situation if he so wished, except Peter saw it as hopeless with all the exits cut off and took the action he did with the sword. But if the scripture were not fulfilled and the things spoken of did not take place, how would the promised redemption come to save mankind? How could sin be defeated unless he died by crucifixion? How could death be defeated unless he rose from the dead on the third day? It was not appropriate to "pray to my Father [to] give me more than twelve legions of angels", for his hour was now come. He would go to the cross. He would not put God to the proof or tempt his Father. The adversary now represented in Peter and his diabolical actions was put behind him, and the temptation firmly repudiated.

The Jewish trials

"Then did they spit in his face, and buffeted him; and others smote him with the palms of their hands, saying, Prophesy unto us, thou Christ, Who is he that smote thee?" (Matthew 26:67,68)

What Matthew does not tell us, but both Mark and Luke do, is that Jesus was blindfolded. Some of those mocking him, and Mark called them "the servants", slapped him. They were playing a guessing game, having sport with the Son of God, 'Who hit you across the face? Name your tormentors!' The record is silent whether Jesus did, but it's doubtful if he would. He could have named his tormentors quite easily. He could sense their twisted minds and bullying thoughts. But he resisted the temptation and the goading. He would not perform a stage variety act to satisfy their corrupt and warped demands, and provide for their amusement. Even if he had revealed the perpetrators, it would not have changed the outcome of the trial, illegal as it was. The sentence would still have been death. He firmly resisted this temptation to do the spectacular, which was identical to the wilderness test to "cast thyself down" from the pinnacle of the temple. Jesus was accused of blasphemy. Luke adds an ironic touch, "Many other things blasphemously spake they against him" (Luke 22:65).

On the cross

The events which occurred at the cross would have tested Jesus to the limit. Although the victory over himself had been won in the Garden of Gethsemane, and he had willingly resolved to accomplish the final stages, this still had to be physically and mentally endured, with all the associated cruelty and humiliation. The taunting by those watching him would have contributed to his pains and anguish:

"And they that passed by reviled him, wagging their heads, and saying, Thou that destroyest the temple, and buildest it in three days, save thyself. If thou be the Son of God, come down from the cross. Likewise also the chief priests mocking him, with the scribes and elders, said, He saved others; himself he cannot save. If he be the King of Israel, let him now come down from the cross, and we will believe him. He trusted in God; let him deliver him now, if he will have him: for he said, I am the Son of God. The thieves also, which were crucified with him, cast the same in his teeth ... The rest said, Let be, let us see whether Elias will come to save him."

(Matthew 27:39-44,49)

This narrative condemns both the leaders and the people, even the two thieves. Every verse in this short section, either specifically or by implication, includes the words "Come down from the cross". The nails wouldn't have held him to the stake, whether there were two, three or four, if he had prayed to his Father for angelic support and deliverance, pleading the promise of Psalm 91. The angels would have come to his aid. He could have been freed and been at the centre of the most impressive act of self-preservation ever seen, and at a most dramatic time. He could have taken the kingdom and the nation by storm, overwhelmed the Jews, and defeated the Romans, all in a moment. But it was not to be.

This was the temptation to leap from the temple pinnacle without comparison. It was rejected. The personal difficulties which were at the heart of the proving of Jesus were compounded by the frequent references by his tormentors to the Psalms, mainly 22 and 69, but including others, as the following table illustrates. It will not be a complete list as other references would likely have been used. The opportunity has been taken to review all the Gospel narratives of the crucifixion.

References to the Psalms at the crucifixion		
Matthew	**Event quoted**	**Psalm**
27:34	Gave him vinegar to drink	69:21
27:35	They crucified him	22:16
27:35	They parted his garments	22:18
27:36	They watched him there	22:17
27:41	Likewise mocking him	22:12,13; 69:12; 71:10
27:43	He trusted in God – let Him deliver him	22:8; 42:10
27:43	He trusted in God	3:3
27:44	The thieves also cast the same in his teeth	35:15; 69:7,26
27:46	My God why hast thou forsaken me?	22:1; 69:17
27:48	Gave him vinegar to drink	69:21
27:50	Yielded up the spirit	22:14,15

Mark	**Event quoted**	**Psalm**
15:23	Drink wine mingled with myrrh	69:21
15:24	They crucified him	22:16,17
15:24	Parted my garments	22:18

15:26	The superscription	76:10 2:6
15:29	Passers-by railed on him, wagging their heads	69:7,19,20, 26; 22:7,8,12, 13; 109:25
15:31	Chief priests mocking said to the scribes	2:1,2
15:34	My God, my God	22:1; 69:17
15:34	Why hast thou forsaken me?	22:1; 27:9; 42:9; 71:11; 69:17
15:36	Vinegar given to drink	69:21

Luke	Event quoted	Psalm
23:33	They crucified him	22:16
23:34	They parted his garments	22:18
23:35	Rulers derided him	22:7; 5:15,19,25; 69:7,20,26; 71:11
23:35	People stood beholding him	2:1; 22:12,13,17
23:36	Soldiers mocked him and offered vinegar	69:21
23:42	Lord remember me	106:4-6
23:42	Come into thy kingdom	2:6,8
23:46	Father I commend my spirit	31:5

John	Event quoted	Psalm
19:18,23	They crucified him	22:16
19:24	They parted my raiment	22:18
19:28	I thirst	22:15; 69:21
19:29	Vinegar put to his mouth	69:21
19:30	It is finished	22:31
19:30	Bowed the head and died	22:15

Both Psalms 22 and 69 are Messianic; that is prophetic of the life, works and death of Christ. Yet this was not understood by those who played out the drama or quoted them so profusely, but so blindly. The psalms shouted out that the crucified one had declared God's name to his people, and that he is the governor among the nations (Psalm 22:22,28) – a clear reference to their Messiah, the Christ.

We shall also explore two other Old Testament references which were quoted by Jesus' enemies, to conclude our consideration of the repetition in the ministry of the 'leap from the pinnacle of the temple' temptation. First we note how many times "save thyself" or "save himself" or the equivalent, occur in the short passage from Matthew 27 which was quoted earlier describing the crucifixion, namely verses 40,42,43,49. The phrase comes from the Old Testament:

"Rejoice greatly, O daughter of Zion; shout, O daughter of Jerusalem: behold, thy King cometh unto thee: he is just, and having salvation; lowly, and riding upon an ass, and upon a colt the foal of an ass." (Zechariah 9:9)

"Having salvation" is shown in the Authorised Version margin as "saving himself", and this is the language of the New Testament passage. The ride into Jerusalem was only five days earlier than the events Matthew describes, and had caused quite a stir among the people and the Pharisees. He had received a wonderful reception and much adulation, but it all evaporated to nothing within this very short period.

The other phrase in verse 42, "If he be the King of Israel" is also of Old Testament origin, and in the prophecy of Zephaniah, although its basis is the Davidic covenant, with Jesus the rightful heir to David's throne. It is also found in Ezekiel's prophecy (21:27).

"Sing, O daughter of Zion; shout, O Israel; be glad and rejoice with all the heart, O daughter of Jerusalem. The LORD hath taken away thy judgments, he hath cast out thine enemy: the king of Israel, even the LORD, is in the midst of thee: thou shalt not see evil any more." (Zephaniah 3:14,15)

We note how verse 14 and the invitation to praise are repeated in Zechariah 9:9.

But verse 15 is concerned with the act of crucifixion and what it would accomplish. It would [1] remove punishments due to sin, [2] destroy death; [3] indicate the presence of the King of Israel in their midst, even though at that precise moment he was "high and lifted up"; [4] guarantee there would be no more suffering or trouble because Christ was victorious, and the people would share in the benefit.

These promising scriptures would undoubtedly flood into the mind of Jesus as he hung on the cross. This was a very difficult situation given the immediate needs of both himself and his people. He was faced with many choices and could have:

- Yielded to temptation and prayed to be freed by the angels.
- Demonstrated he was the fulfilment of Psalm 22 – did they not hear him saying the prayer and reciting the psalm?

- Reminded them of the entry into Jerusalem on the ass and their adulation less than week earlier as spoken by the prophet.
- Explained he was the promised King of Israel, the descendant and inheritor of David's throne, based on Zephaniah's message.
- Said how his crucifixion was an integral part of that process, so he must have been their Messiah and King.

All these things when combined brought Jesus once more face to face with the second temptation to leap from the pinnacle of the temple, to extricate himself from the cross and demonstrate his divine origin. He could do the impressive stunt and exercise the pride of life. He could escape the cross finally to convince them, once and for all time, of who he was, the Son of God, their Christ, their King. But he didn't. He firmly rejected the temptation. He didn't call on twelve legions of angels as had been promised, for his time, his "hour" was now come. The Lord Jesus was totally victorious and in control of the situation. He overcame all his natural fleshly inclinations to save himself, and followed the divine principle of unquestioning and absolute faith in the word and will of his Father. "Into thy hands I commend my spirit" (Psalm 31:5, Luke 23:46).

14

PRAY THAT YOU ENTER NOT INTO TEMPTATION

THE temptation to take all the kingdoms of the world was not just about kingship. It was also about power, the accolades of subjects, worship by the people, being a ruler and a judge. This was the lust of the eyes, the desire for dominion, influence and control. As the temple pinnacle temptation was real and forceful, so was the invitation to take "all the kingdoms of the world". This could be the most spectacular, as nation after nation and kingdom after kingdom would fall under the control of the greatest man who had ever lived, and who would have unlimited power. What else would he need to do to prove his claims that he was the Son of God, Israel's promised Christ, their King? How the Jews would rally to his side, as the hated Romans were first subdued, then dominated, then defeated, then ejected from the land! This was the prospect, but it was also the test. The promise of his kingship over "all the Gentiles" was unbreakable. He had supporters, a land, a law enshrined in the scriptures and a capital city. All he needed was a grand entrance and he would have everything.

'Just fall down and worship me and all is yours', said the tempter. 'Do your own thing, be yourself, take what is rightfully yours. Why do you wait? Think of all the good you could do, if you had the kingdom now'. This would sound very plausible, but it was very superficial when closely examined, and was seen to be all false and deceptive. For the voice did not say, 'It will only last for your natural lifetime until you die and then it will be all over. But it will be great while it lasts!' The serpent was at work and the temptation was put.

I have selected four incidents to show the repetition of this temptation in the ministry: (1) an identity crisis; {2} the transfiguration; (3) the tribute money; and (4) Jesus the King of the Jews – the accusation before both the Jewish and Roman courts.

An identity crisis

"And it came to pass, as he was alone praying, his disciples were with him: and he asked them, saying, Whom say the people that I am? They answering said, John the Baptist; but some say, Elias; and others say, that one of the old prophets is risen again. He said unto them, But whom say you that I am? Peter answering said, The Christ of God. And he straitly charged them, and commanded them to tell no man that thing; saying, The Son of man must suffer many things, and be rejected of the elders and chief priests and scribes, and be slain, and be raised the third day." (Luke 9:18-22)

This conversation followed the feeding of the five thousand. It was just a year to the cross. He was praying alone. We'll discover why in a moment. There was still some confusion about who Jesus was, and still an identity crisis even after two-and-a-half years of public service. The people thought Jesus to be either John the Baptist, Elijah or one of the prophets "risen from dead". Not so. What did the twelve think? That was crucial for him to know. Were they as confused as the people? Peter's answer was clear. It was a firm declaration of faith on behalf of them all: "The Christ of God!"

This event has its parallels with John's record, as follows:

"From that time many of his disciples went back, and walked no more with him. Then said Jesus unto the twelve, Will you also go away? Then Simon Peter answered him, Lord, to whom shall we go? Thou hast the words of eternal life. And we believe and are sure

that thou art that Christ, the Son of the living God."
(John 6:66-69)

John 6 is the discourse on the bread of life, which was the exhortation after feeding the five thousand the day before. Jesus' miracle had been misunderstood, and now "they would come and take him by force, to make him king" (verse 15). He departed into a mountain himself alone, to pray. It was this temptation to make him king that drove him away, for the tempter was enticing him, 'the kingdom is yours – take it'. The pressure was now coming from the people desperate for relief and release from oppression, both secular and religious. They saw in Jesus the ideal candidate to be their king. Who else could provide so much for so many from so little? This is why he departed alone to pray: to find the strength to resist the pressure, and to focus on his ultimate purpose as "the Lamb of God, which taketh away the sin of the world".

This must have been a disappointing time for Jesus, that his encouragement for the people in providing more than enough to feed them, and his sermon explaining the spiritual significance of the bread and the kind of lives he would wish them to lead, was so misunderstood or deliberately set aside, because of the challenges he made to their personal lives. His exhortation had focused on himself as "the bread of life" that a man must eat to live forever. "This is a hard saying", they declared, "Who can hear it?" As a consequence many drifted away (verse 66). There is just the hint, when we read between the lines and get into the emotion and reality of the occasion, that there was the provocation to 'go for it', to remedy a deteriorating situation. Support was ebbing away, and it might have been felt that after two-and-a-half years of hard work the ministry was turning out to be a failure.

The conversation between Jesus and the twelve, as we have it in Luke 9, is filled out here in John 6. "Will ye also go away?" Was this Jesus at a low point? He had fed five thousand but they had drifted away.

169

It seemed that Jesus was in danger of being isolated and left with only a few companions, however fickle their support might be. Peter's answer (verses 68,69), "We believe and are sure that thou art that Christ, the Son of the living God", is picked up from the teaching of Psalm 2, where Jesus is described as "My Son", "my king upon my holy hill of Zion". How easily this difficult situation could have been changed. The people wanted him as their king. He could be their king! It could all be changed in a moment. But any thoughts of 'going for it' and declaring spectacularly who and what he was, were put to one side and denied. "His hour was not yet come".

The transfiguration

"And after six days Jesus taketh Peter, James, and John his brother, and bringeth them up into an high mountain apart, and was transfigured before them: and his face did shine as the sun, and his raiment was white as the light ... While he yet spake, behold, a bright cloud overshadowed them: and behold a voice out of the cloud, which said, This is my beloved Son, in whom I am well pleased; hear ye him."

(Matthew 17:1,2,5)

The transfiguration was about two-and-a-half years into the ministry. It was around twelve months to the cross, and in the same time frame as the identity crisis we have just considered.

This unique event confirms the Sonship of Jesus through an experience of resurrection and kingdom glory, with its references to Psalm 2 and Isaiah 42. The description of his transformed state is duplicated in the New Testament by the two angels who were in the empty tomb on the resurrection morning. Did Jesus temporarily take on the nature of angels, that excel in strength, as the ministers of God, that do His pleasure, made as spirits, and like flaming fire? This was a time that was truly 'other worldly'. To discover how the transfiguration occurred is not my purpose. We accept that it happened as described. Jesus was exalted to glory, which could only mean his kingship and the kingdom, immortality and incorruptibility. He would qualify for kingship. The voice from heaven spoke approval, as it had already done at his baptism, hinting at the prophecy of Isaiah 42 and the prospects of Psalm 2. Peter was there as a witness, but in a state of wonderment and worship, and also "sore afraid". It made a great impact on him as it must have done on James and John. Peter wrote about this profound event as follows:

"For we ... were eyewitnesses of his majesty. For he received from God the Father honour and glory, when there came such a voice to him from the excellent glory, This is my beloved Son, in whom I am well pleased. And this voice which came from heaven we heard, when we were with him in the holy mount." (2 Peter 1:16-18)

Peter's language leaves us in no doubt about what he saw, and what the transfiguration was intended to convey to the disciples who were present, and to Jesus. Peter wrote of "his majesty", meaning the King himself or the associated glory and honour, or even both. Jesus received "honour and glory", when the voice from heaven came to him.

The word "came" (Greek, *phero*) in verses 17 and 18 means to bear, or to carry, and can convey the sense of powerful activity. This has a relationship to 'spirit', by which we mean breath, wind or word that is God-breathed, an inspired activity. We could read the verses in the following way, in order to understand the activity which was taking place and the energy being released at this unique time: "when there was borne to him such a voice" (verse 17), and "this voice which was borne from heaven we heard" (verse 18). Peter is indicating that he experienced the activity of the word of God in "the holy mount".

If Peter and presumably James and John experienced this, how much more powerful was it for Jesus who was at the heart of this spirit activity and transformation? Kingship and all its associated prospects had been confirmed and granted in a powerful awe-inspiring way. There had been the angelic-type appearance, revelation by the law and the prophets, spirit activity, the voice from heaven, a holy mount, resurrection, kingship, honour and glory. It was a majestic endorsement of his present life and future role. He was the King of the world, by right, by inheritance and promise from the highest authority.

The temptation to capitalise on this divine personal testimony could well have been present, especially when he reached the lower slopes of the mountain and the crowds seeking healing, with their complaints about the failure of the other disciples to cure the epileptic boy. He went from the exalted heights charged with glory, honour and eternity, to the valley of the shadow of disease and death in a few short steps. How frustrating and disappointing, naturally speaking. How he could have used his power for good! His homily on the disciples' inability to heal is recorded in Matthew 17:20,21. These verses could well be references back to the wilderness temptations, and how he was occupied and triumphed during the forty days with prayer and fasting.

Tribute money

There were plenty of incidents to remind Jesus that he was the King of the Jews by inheritance as well as by promise. The tribute money is a case in point:

"And when they were come to Capernaum, they that received the tribute money came to Peter, and said, Doth not your master pay tribute? He saith, Yes. And when he was come into the house, Jesus prevented him, saying, What thinkest thou, Simon? of whom do the kings of the earth take custom or tribute? of their own children, or of strangers? Peter saith unto him, Of strangers. Jesus saith unto him, Then are the children free. Notwithstanding, lest we should offend them, go thou to the sea, and cast an hook, and take up the fish that first cometh up; and when thou hast opened his mouth, thou shalt find a piece of money: that take, and give unto them for me and thee." (Matthew 17:24-27)

This is about the Jews' own internal tax system. Roman taxes collected by publicans like Matthew and Zacchaeus were in addition. The tribute money was a temple tax of half a shekel per person, like a poll tax. It should only have been collected during or after a periodic population census, but Jewish practice had made it an annual event. Peter's answer in verse 25 indicates that Jesus had paid this tax before. On this occasion he anticipated Peter and asked him a question, which teaches us about his regard for the civil and religious authorities, for kings and governors, and therefore our acknowledgement of present day national governments and local councils, whatever the politics or the justice of their laws and governance.

"Them", in the dialogue between Jesus and Peter, are the kings of the earth who receive the tribute, the temple tax. This was collected by the Jewish religious authority which had the Sanhedrin as its power base. Therefore, the members of the Sanhedrin in this case are the kings of the earth because they held the religious sway over the people. It was a tax for the house of God. Those who paid it were "strangers", because tax was collected from "strangers". Therefore the taxpayers by this definition were the strangers before God, a relationship which would be denied by them, because they would have said they were the "children". Jesus however said they were strangers, because their faith and works were not those of their father Abraham. The enforcement of the annual tax emphasised the nation's bondage to the law and their consequent estrangement from God. They were still slaves to sin and death when they could have been made free by faith in Christ. Jesus' answer was "lest we should offend them". That was why he paid the tax, and he is clearly implying he needn't have done! Why? Because both he and Peter were the true children of God by faith and therefore free. They were not the strangers. As free children they were not under any obligation to pay the tax. Jesus obviously considered that his Sonship and Peter's faith qualified them both to be "children" and "free".

Jesus' example is a good lesson for us about our duty to the civil authorities, and our obligation to pay "tribute to whom tribute is due; custom to whom custom; fear to whom fear; honour to whom honour" (Romans 13:7). This is because our calling to the Gospel, our citizenship being in heaven, qualifies us to be the children of God, and therefore by our profession of faith we are "strangers and pilgrims on the earth"; sojourners having "no continuing city". We are under a greater duty than our neighbours to pay our taxes, because the kings of the earth collect their taxes from strangers, which we are, whereas our neighbours are "the children and free", in this present dispensation.

One other element calls for comment: "Of whom do the kings of the earth take custom or tribute? of their own children or of strangers?" Jesus is *the* King of the earth by right, by appointment and promise. He was higher than all those in office: the High Priest, Chief Priests, the Sanhedrin, the Pharisees, Sadducees, Herod, Pontius Pilate, the Emperor. Because the tax was collected for the temple, and this was his Father's house, the nation should really have been paying their tribute to him, as they were the strangers to God, until by faith in him they became his children and free. But Jesus did not press this for "his hour was not yet come", and "lest we should offend them". The tax was paid.

The temptation to hold back the payment of the tax, in order to exert his true position as the only and beloved Son of God, claim his kingdom and his people together with the land, might have been lying dormant: for the proper use of the temple of God was being abused, it had turned into "a den of thieves" and a place for corrupt money changers; also because he was *the* King of all the earth, and particularly the King of Israel, as well as being the Son of the House. But all this was repudiated. The tempter was defeated. The danger passed.

Jesus – the King of the Jews

As the end of his natural life drew nearer, so the matter of Jesus being the promised King of the Jews received even more prominence, and never more so than during the trials, both Jewish and Roman.

"Jesus of Nazareth the King of the Jews" was one of the accusations levelled against him and eventually the Jewish elders successfully persuaded Pilate of the legitimacy of their cause. They argued that his claim to be the King of Israel was treason against Caesar and the Roman state. "We have no king but Caesar", was to prove their undoing in AD 70.

(a) The Jewish trial

"And as soon as it was day, the elders of the people and the chief priests and the scribes came together, and led him into their council, saying, Art thou the Christ? tell us. And he said unto them, If I tell you, ye will not believe: and if I also ask you, ye will not answer me, nor let me go. Hereafter shall the Son of man sit on the right hand of the power of God. Then said they all, Art thou then the Son of God? And he said unto them, Ye say that I am." (Luke 22:66-70)

The cross-questioning by the religious judges began with a question about his kingship, 'Are you the Christ, the Messiah, the Anointed, the promised King of the Jews?' Jesus' response confirmed that he was, by quoting from two Old Testament prophecies, namely Daniel 7 and Psalm 110. His answer must have prompted them to make some connections and come to an understanding of the prophecies, for the Sanhedrin's next question had its basis in Psalm 2, 'Are you then the Son of God?', as if it was so self-evident from the two scriptures he must be. Each of these three passages is about him being 'the King'. Importantly, Jesus' answer showed that being the King over the kingdom of the Jews was very much at the forefront of his thinking, even at this critical moment of his trial.

175

We shall briefly look now at Daniel 7, Psalm 110 and Psalm 2 which were central to Jesus' claims and his answers to the inquisitors.

The Son of man – Daniel 7

"Behold, one like the Son of man came with the clouds of heaven, and came to the Ancient of days, and they brought him near before him. And there was given him dominion, and glory, and a kingdom, that all people, nations, and languages, should serve him: his dominion is an everlasting dominion, which shall not pass away, and his kingdom that which shall not be destroyed." (Daniel 7:13,14)

So the title Son of man is not just or even mainly about Jesus being the natural born human son of Mary. It is a reference to him as the representative man of the right hand, the Son of man made strong for God (Psalm 80:17); and the firstborn of a new creation, higher than the kings of the earth (Psalm 89:27). The Daniel passage is about kingdom glory and the fulfilment of all hopes, when other powers and authorities are put down. Jesus would understand that he was at the heart of this prophecy. His Jewish enemies would know that this passage was a promise concerning the work of their Messiah at the time of the future glory of their nation. Jesus would also know that the power which was represented by Pontius Pilate, and which opposed him, was written into this same Daniel 7 passage at verses 7 and 19, as well as 8:24.

Sitting at the right hand of God – Psalm 110

"The LORD said unto my Lord, Sit thou at my right hand, until I make thine enemies thy footstool. The LORD shall send the rod of thy strength out of Zion: rule thou in the midst of thine enemies." (Psalm 110:1,2)

Here is a plain reference to the King, his authority, to his being the conqueror, overcoming his enemies, ruling them and the people with righteousness and equity. His assertion that he would sit at the right hand of the God of heaven, however, fuelled the charge of blasphemy. Yet the claim was true. This passage had already been a matter of discussion between Jesus and the Pharisees (Matthew 22:41-45), when he said, "If David then call him Lord, how is he his son?" Their inability to answer put the seal on any further questioning in the ministry. But it meant that the matter of Jesus' divine person and his origins had become a live issue once more.

Yet there had been no appeal to Jesus to explain what this passage did mean; for had they asked, his explanation would have compromised their standing, straightened out their warped thinking, and removed one of the main planks of their accusations. Their case against him would have collapsed.

"Art thou then the Son of God?" – Psalm 2

Psalm 2 had been the basis for the wilderness temptation to take "all the kingdoms of the world". There could hardly be a plainer reference in the whole of the Old Testament to the Son of God:

> "Yet have I set my king upon my holy hill of Zion. I will declare the decree: the LORD hath said unto me, Thou art my Son; this day have I begotten thee. Ask of me, and I shall give thee the heathen for thine inheritance, and the uttermost parts of the earth for thy possession." (Psalm 2:6-8)

Again, here are the strongest of indications about his kingship, together with Zion the place of holiness, Yahweh speaking to His Son, the promise of the Gentile nations as a gift and his own worldwide domination. Above all this, it is the source of the words spoken from heaven at both his baptism and the transfiguration, which the religious leaders could not fail to have heard about.

When we consider that Jesus was the King, and had the authority and the power to bring about radical changes to his world, there was probably a return or remembrance of 'All this power will I give you and the glory of them. If you worship me, all will be yours'. But

177

the temptation to take his inheritance prematurely was denied. "His hour was not yet come."

(b) The Roman trial

Jesus' appearance before Pilate may well have been another occasion when the temptation to take "all the kingdoms of the world" could have become a live issue, in view of the things said about him and those done to him. The question of his being a king and having a kingdom was put before the Roman court as a reason why Jesus should be put to death. But this time the Jewish accusation appeared to have misfired.

During the Roman trial, Jesus told Pilate:

> "My kingdom is not of this world: if my kingdom were of this world, then would my servants fight, that I should not be delivered to the Jews: but now is my kingdom not from hence." (John 18:36)

Jesus did not deny that he was a king, or that he could command a kingdom. But he did deny that it was there and then, and deferred it to some future time. Was it this confession which persuaded Pilate to write the superscription over the cross, "This is Jesus of Nazareth the King of the Jews"? Pilate must have been persuaded of the truth of this claim, despite the Jews' insistence that the wording should be changed to, "He said, I am King of the Jews". Pilate's most authoritative reply put an end to the matter. "What I have written I have written". Although Pilate seems to have been ambivalent about Jesus' claims, it could be debated whether Pilate believed them or not; or he considered Jesus was deluded but harmless and therefore innocent; or whether his final decision was political. But others were there who would exploit these claims for their own amusement:

> "And they [the soldiers] stripped him, and put on him a scarlet robe. And when they had platted a crown of thorns, they put it upon his head, and a reed in his right hand: and they bowed the knee before him, and mocked him, saying, Hail, King of the Jews!" (Matthew 27:28,29)

178

This is a desperate scene. Soldiers not knowing or caring what they did or who he was, were having a game of sport as they mocked and abused the King of the Jews. The sport was cruel and hideous. The gentle and innocent man was at the mercy of rough and crude soldiers. But the King was as dignified as he could be.

The office of kingship – according to the soldiers Matthew 27	
:28	A scarlet robe – colour of a king's garments – double sided. Mark 15:17-19 describes it as "purple" – his robe
:29	Thorns on his head – his crown
:29	The reed in the right hand – his sceptre of regal authority and office
:29	Soldiers bowed their knees – Mark adds "worshipped him"
:29	They mocked him – Mark adds they "salute him"
:29	They acclaim him – "Hail, King of the Jews"

After this 'dressing up' game the mood changes dramatically to their spitting and beating, and his humiliation and pain. These were difficult moments for Jesus as the King of the Jews, for this was a re-run of the wilderness temptation, "all this power will I give thee". Except now, the Romans were 'worshipping' Jesus, but insincerely and with much mockery, born out of boredom and the consumption of cheap common wine. Yet three-and-a-half years earlier, the tempter had invited Jesus to bow the knee and worship, and all the kingdoms of the world would be his.

The answer, then as now, was the same, "Get thee behind me, Satan: for it is written, Thou shalt worship

179

the Lord thy God, and him only shalt thou serve". All thought of self-preservation was discounted and denied. He was victorious. He courageously bore the reproach of those who counted as nothing his Father's purpose.

The Old Testament gives us a flavour of the intensity of these moments during his trials. Psalm 39 is a snapshot of what was happening. There are references to bridling the tongue, being dumb with silence, understanding the brevity of natural life, the inevitability of death, a recognition that all was in the hands and control of his Father. For example:

"I said, I will take heed to my ways, that I sin not with my tongue: I will keep my mouth with a bridle, while the wicked is before me. I was dumb with silence, I held my peace, even from good; and my sorrow was stirred. My heart was hot within me, while I was musing the fire burned: then spake I with my tongue, LORD, make me to know mine end, and the measure of my days, what it is; that I may know how frail I am." (Psalm 39:1-4)

These verses express the feelings and thoughts of Jesus as outrageous things and unjust attitudes were manifested against him. The silence he kept; the hot emotion he felt; the silently uttered prayer of verse 4. This was not resignation, but strong resolve to remain in total control of the events and himself. This was an occasion when the flesh would be at its strongest, rebelling against the injustices and the rage meted out to him. But the spirit was even stronger.

Consider verse 3, "My heart was hot within me". Aren't we being told there was a welling up of emotion, perhaps even of anger or frustration, as if something burned within him, and demanded a response and a rebuff, naturally speaking? But "I held my peace, even from good". Then he spoke a prayer to his Father, silently in the heart. It quelled the fire and cooled the heat within him. The prayer is about the worth of human nature, and the frailty and brevity of life, even that of Jesus himself.

180

"And now, LORD, what wait I for? my hope is in thee. Deliver me from all my transgressions: make me not the reproach of the foolish. I was dumb, I opened not my mouth; because thou didst it."

(verses 7-9)

This section which is the prayer and meditation of the Son seems to be saying, 'Your purpose is coming to its end. I am part of it. My hope is with you. Deliver me out of all this evil. End the reproaches. I remained silent, because this work is yours. You did it. You brought me to the way of the cross.' "It pleased the LORD to bruise him", the prophet was to confirm. So the Lord Jesus suffered the indignities and resisted the temptation by which he could have escaped all this abuse, and which would have made absolutely clear his position as the King of the Jews with all the associated power. The Lord was triumphant.

I have attempted to show from across the four Gospels that the wilderness temptations represented by (1) turning the stones into bread (2) leaping off the pinnacle of the temple, and (3) taking all the kingdoms of the world, as manifestations of the lust of the flesh and of the eyes and the pride of life, never left Jesus. These three temptations were continually with him in one form or another, plaguing him, testing him and proving him 'whether he would keep the commandments of his Father or not'. He had been triumphant and the victory was his. His own self had been denied. So he was humbled and had learned that he did not live by bread alone, but by every word that proceeded from his Father. He had learned that God is to be feared, and not to be deliberately or foolishly put to the proof, to deliver what He had promised. He had learned too that God is to be worshipped even at the expense of himself if need be, whatever the cost, if his service was going to glorify God and further His purpose of redemption.

15

LEAD ME NOT INTO TEMPTATION

WE begin another voyage of discovery as we endeavour to discover the possible ways in which Jesus secured his victory over the innumerable temptations he faced. It is an attempt to explore and reconstruct the principles which guided and encouraged Jesus in his living, and which put paid to "the wiles of the devil". We have journeyed with him so far as closely as we could, and have seen how he wrestled with his adversary the tempter in the wilderness, and then on many occasions fought the same battles again during his ministry. This journey too will be as reverent as possible.

Jesus was very sensitive to sin and all possible wrongdoing by himself. He struggled and agonised because of the pressures on him, and "offered up prayers and supplications with strong crying and tears unto him that was able to save him from death" (Hebrews 5:7). His eventual victory was not easily accomplished. It caused him considerable pain day by day.

He constantly turned to prayer to find the strength to deal with the difficult situations and confrontations as they challenged him, his faith and integrity, but above all, his loyalty and obedience which had been promised to his Father. He was savaged mentally and physically by his enemies, but took no revenge, as he knew that "all things are naked and opened unto the eyes of him with whom he had to do" (4:13), and also that "Vengeance is mine; I will repay, saith the Lord" (Romans 12:19). He left all these matters in his Father's hands. Meanwhile he suffered. He knew the prophet's words, "Thou art of purer eyes than to behold evil, and canst not look on iniquity" (Habakkuk 1:13), and may have wondered why God was so longsuffering with the wicked. But his work was to be a righteous Saviour, so "he made himself of no reputation ... humbled himself and [was] obedient" (Philippians 2:7,8).

Divine education

"And the spirit of the LORD shall rest upon him, the spirit of wisdom and understanding, the spirit of counsel and might, the spirit of knowledge and of the fear of the LORD; and shall make him of quick understanding in the fear of the LORD: and he shall not judge after the sight of his eyes, neither reprove after the hearing of his ears."　　　(Isaiah 11:2,3)

Isaiah wrote prophetically of the spirit of the Lord resting upon him, that spirit of wisdom, understanding, counsel and might, and of knowledge and the fear of the Lord. But these were his qualities and personal attributes, the building blocks which formed his character. They were learned in and by the experiences of life, and from the instruction of his Father, as Isaiah 50 so beautifully and delicately describes:

"The Lord GOD has given me the tongue of the learned, that I should know how to speak a word in season to him that is weary: he wakeneth morning by morning, he wakeneth mine ear to hear as the learned."　　　(Isaiah 50:4)

This was the Father's response to his Son's prayers of faith for support, strength and guidance. This was to know and have confirmed again, the Father's loving-kindness. This was how Jesus, amongst other ways, knew the ways of God, learned His graciousness and mercy, longsuffering and truth. He learned how to overcome the flesh and promote the spirit, so that the word in season to the weary was always on his lips. He realised because of the wilderness temptation experiences, that a man shall live by every word which proceeds out of the mouth of God. The daily lesson of divine principles absorbed by the Son as he sat at his Father's feet, was the education that prepared him for even greater things. He was not a rebellious son, nor would he go back on what he had promised. He was obedient and faithful. There was a spiritual development in the things of the word, as he grew from boyhood to manhood, which gave substance to and enhanced his inclination to God's ways. There was the strongest of bonds with his Father.

Consequently it is not reasonable to conclude that he was born with the qualities which Isaiah 11 describes, so that they provided him with an inbuilt immunity to temptation or even possible wrongdoing, and therefore he automatically had all the right answers to the different questions, problems and difficulties he faced. If this were the case, he could not have been challenged in those things which give us our greatest concerns, that is, our temptations and the ever present susceptibility to do wrong. He would have had a distinct advantage, meaning he could not fully identify with our nature. The resistance he showed and the wisdom he demonstrated was learned in the hard school of experience in the Jewish world. These qualities were first honed during the hidden years at Nazareth, which gave him the essential early skills to make him of "quick understanding in the fear of the LORD", as his question and answer session in the temple with the doctors of the law at the age of twelve clearly shows.

The Revised Version gives this last phrase as, "his delight shall be in the fear of the LORD", and the *Companion Bible* offers, "the reverence of Jehovah shall be fragrance to him". This wording is supported by the Authorised Version margin, which refers to his understanding and fear as a sweet "smell", or "scent" – as incense before the Lord. His thoughts and actions were seen by his Father as acceptable acts of worship and devotion, the sweet smell of incense.

These qualities and characteristics, his delight in the ways and the fear of the Lord, coupled with his delightful and exemplary life in the eyes of his Father, enabled him to make judgements and take decisions that were quite uncommon, and not after man. He possessed an insight and an intimate knowledge of his fellows and of himself that meant he could set aside judgements after "the sight of his eyes" and "the hearing of his ears". He had a faculty which enabled him to read the hearts and motives of friends as well as adversaries. This must have been quite a burden to carry.

It is possible to trace the qualities of Isaiah 11:2,3 in the New Testament as Jesus' life developed. For example Luke, in describing those hidden years at Nazareth tells us more about Jesus' spiritual development than his natural (see 2:40-52). He became strong in spirit and outlook; he showed discernment and judgement, because he was filled with a wisdom which came from above. The care and devotion of his heavenly Father rested upon him because of his own devotional attention to the things of God. In the eighteen years of silence, this spiritual wisdom blossomed into maturity, as the Lord himself grew up before his Father as a tender plant.

Commenting on the opening verses of Isaiah 11, one writer observed that "to begin with, there is the geography of a royal mind in its stretches of character, knowledge and achievement". He continues:

"The second verse is the definition of this character; the third describes the atmosphere in which it lives. 'And there shall rest upon him the Spirit of Jehovah, the spirit of wisdom and understanding, the spirit of counsel and might, the spirit of knowledge and the fear of Jehovah; and he shall draw breath in the fear of Jehovah' – in other words, ripeness but also sharpness of mind; moral decision and heroic energy; piety in its two forms of knowing the will of God and feeling the constraint to perform it. We could not have a more concise summary of the strong elements of a ruling mind."[1]

This same writer also offers an alternative form of words for the first part of verse 3:

1 George Adam Smith, *The Book of Isaiah*, Volume 1, page 181, 9th edition, 1896.

"If the Old Testament has a phrase for sinlessness, that phrase occurs here, in the beginning of the third verse. In the Authorised English Version it is translated, 'and shall make him of quick understanding in the fear of the Lord' and in the Revised Version, 'His delight shall be in the fear of the Lord' ... But the phrase may as well mean, 'He shall draw his breath in the fear of the Lord'; and it is a great pity, that our revisers have not even on the margin given to English readers any suggestion of so picturesque, and probably so correct, a rendering. It is a most expressive definition of sinlessness – sinlessness which was the attribute of Christ alone ... He was his own atmosphere, 'drawing breath in the fear of the Lord'. Of him alone it is recorded, that, though living in the world, he was never infected with the world's sin. The blast of no man's cruelty ever kindled unholy wrath within his breast; nor did men's unbelief carry to his soul its deadly chill. Not even when he was led of the devil into the atmosphere of temptation, did his heart throb with one rebellious ambition. Christ 'drew breath in the fear of the Lord'."[2]

This is a description of a sensitive mind attuned to the holiness of heaven, but living in and experiencing the harshness of the earthy with all its brutality and inflaming passions. The LXX reads: "and godliness shall fill him", which expresses his disposition to the way of the spirit and the devout and holy life. This was a serious commitment to a serious call.

If the question is asked in the light of these testimonies, 'Just how did Jesus achieve his victory over temptation – what was his secret?' the answer has to be, 'We don't really know'. We cannot understand the strength of mind or the absolute single-mindedness which drove Jesus on. He had a capacity for 'locking on' to his ultimate objective and never releasing his grip. This focus and strong-mindedness baffles our weak

2   Ibid, pages 183,184.

human hearts and minds so that we are left marvelling at his dedication for the things of God, motivated by an infinite self-sacrificing love for his Father.

The only begotten Son

Notwithstanding what has been written so far about Jesus' communications with his Father in heaven through his prayers and meditations, and his understanding of the scriptures of truth, there is another aspect we must not forget – the matter of his miraculous birth.

God, the Uncreate Eternal Almighty Maker of the vast and limitless universe is the Father of Jesus. That in itself is a remarkable thing. That God should choose from all the "thousands of Judah" a young virgin daughter of Zion, overshadow her with the power of the Holy Spirit that she should conceive and give birth to the Saviour of the world, is truly wonderful. The loving relationship which existed between the Father and Son is hinted at in scripture, but the curtain remains drawn over the richness of it for the most part. This in the days of his flesh was private and personal. The Son benefitted from sharing the wisdom from above and in return responded with devoted faith expressed in loving obedience.

Matthew, in announcing this momentous event to the Jewish world, described the child of the virgin as "Emmanuel ... God with us" (1:23). This is God acting and meeting the needs of a desperately sick human society by revealing Himself as intimately as possible in His own Son, and offering His own solution to a grave human problem. Consequently as we consider the Son, we see the Father. But it is not always as plain and apparent as we would like. Even the closest companions of Jesus at times were unsure and confused about him, as the following passage makes clear:

"Jesus said, Have I been so long time with you, and yet hast thou not known me, Philip? he that hath seen me hath seen the Father; and how sayest thou then, Show us the Father? Believest thou not that I

187

am in the Father, and the Father in me?"

(John 14:9,10)

This is a unique situation which will never be replicated by any other, as well as a special revelation we are privileged to enter into and understand, albeit faintly.

We come closest possibly to the depth of the Father-Son relationship when we consider Philippians 2:6-8:

"[Jesus], being in the form of God, thought it not robbery to be equal with God: but made himself of no reputation, and took upon him the form of a servant, and was made in the likeness of men: and being found in fashion as a man, he humbled himself, and became obedient unto death, even the death of the cross." (Philippians 2:6-8)

We are inclined to emphasise the humility of Jesus when we expound these three verses and that is quite right. But the language of verse 6 is quite definite: Jesus was "in the form of God". That is, he was the outward appearance of God, having been born by the operation of the Holy Spirit, and in his living delighted to manifest the qualities and love of God his Father. Other renderings explain that Jesus had the status, rank and standing of God – not in any way supporting the doctrine of the Trinity or a pre-existent Christ, but that he represented God, and displayed God's characteristics. "I proceeded forth and came from God" (John 8:42) was the way Jesus put it. He also said, "I and my Father are one" (John 10:30). The Greek for "one" is *hen*. This is neuter, meaning one in essence, union and concord, but not one in substance or one in person. That would require the Greek word to be *heis*, which is masculine.

These passages in John touch on the Father-Son relationship – a closeness of thought and manifestation that is almost too profound to express adequately. It was deep, rich and supportive. Yet for all this, "he thought it not robbery to be equal with God". But equality was there for the taking. The words of the verse say this. If it was not robbery to be equal, then it must have been in order to be equal with God, for the reasons given above. Yet it was not appropriate that he should be equal as he had been sent as the Saviour born "of a woman, made under the law", to redeem mankind from sin and death. He had been tested earlier in the wilderness in this very thing, as we have been exploring in these studies. He had learned and triumphantly declared that "man doth not live by bread only, but by every word that proceedeth out of the mouth of the LORD" (Deuteronomy 8:3). He would not repeat the mistake of Adam and Eve when they grasped at equality with God and paid the ultimate penalty, even though he had an entitlement to do so. Therefore, "he took upon him the form of a servant, and was made in the likeness of men", and was "made ... sin for us, who knew no sin".

Nevertheless, "God was in Christ, reconciling the world unto himself ... that we might be made the righteousness of God in him" (2 Corinthians 5:19,21). There was no other way for man's salvation to be accomplished. No other man could have done what Jesus did, for the simple reason that no other man had God as his Father. It is this and the singular nature of the work he did and how he went about it that makes Jesus unique.

God's solution

What did God do to ensure the salvation of mankind and to restore the glory of His name in all the earth? The prophet Isaiah has a short but impressive series of passages which describe God's apparent dilemma, His solution and His appeal for His creation to turn to Him for redemption. The first is this:

> "Wherefore, when I came, was there no man? when I called, was there none to answer? Is my hand shortened at all, that it cannot redeem? or have I no power to deliver?" (Isaiah 50:2)

This is a direct challenge to us all that we cannot save ourselves, whereas God, notwithstanding our sins and waywardness, is able to do all that is necessary. In the later verses of the chapter He declares His power

189

and willingness to save by describing His terrible acts of judgement on the Egyptians in order to redeem an earlier generation. He reveals the kind of man He would provide and the response His servant would give Him to enable salvation to be accomplished.

Again, here is another statement of God's willingness to work for mankind's good in spite of our separation:

> "Behold, the LORD's hand is not shortened, that it cannot save; neither his ear heavy, that it cannot hear: but your iniquities have separated between you and your God, and your sins have hid his face from you, that he will not hear."   (Isaiah 59:1,2)

This passage reinforces God's intention; His insistence that He is both able and willing to save us despite what had happened in the past which separated us from Him. He could overcome that. His hand was not shortened that it could not save. No one and nothing was forthcoming from mankind to engage with God and bring about the salvation needed. So God of necessity acted independently and arranged for the miraculous begettal of His Son. But we must not overlook the willing involvement of the young virgin from Nazareth who was cruelly "spoken against", and felt "a sword ... pierce through [her] own soul also". Again:

> "And he saw that there was no man, and wondered that there was no intercessor: therefore his arm brought salvation unto him; and his righteousness, it sustained him."   (Isaiah 59:16)

This was a triumphant moment in human history. It was pivotal as it was to reverse the besetting problem that benighted all men and women. "His arm", in addition to taking "the form of a servant", was to be a spiritual warrior and do battle with the sin power unto death. Yet the enormity of the task had been foreseen. Therefore:

> "Let thy hand be upon the man of thy right hand, upon the son of man whom thou madest strong for thyself."   (Psalm 80:17)

Unless he had been made strong, and helped in some undisclosed way by his Father, the prospect of victory must have been in doubt. Without his divine Sonship, salvation could not have been accomplished. But in saying this, we must put aside any suggestion that God did any of the work for Jesus. All victories were solely by the Son.

A unique Son

This means that Jesus was a unique person: the Son of God by Spirit birth and a holy child of promise; but he was also of our nature and son of Mary by natural birth. He had access to divine wisdom and to a source of knowledge and guidance that mere mortal man does not have – or the capacity to grasp in its fullness or even come anywhere near to appreciating. He prayed intensely, consistently and continuously to his all-powerful Spirit-bound and energised Father with whom nothing is impossible. He had immeasurable faith in his Father's words and promises. We too are encouraged to pray and have faith. Yet there is such a chasm between his achievements and our best endeavours; between what he expected his prayers and faith to yield, and what ours actually do. The two cannot be compared; they are too far apart.

This makes him such a wonderful man and Lord. The more we consider what he did, with what he was and what he had, we marvel that so much was done for so many in so short a time, in this one solitary life. But his Father was the Uncreate, without rival in His boundless universe, possessing unlimited power and knowledge.

The issue has been described thus:

"Every man before and since Christ has sinned; that is, has been overcome of sin and is personally a transgressor. If this is so, and it is, how was it possible for Christ, who was fully of our nature, to be different from all other men by remaining sinless? Did he do what other men could have done had they gone about it the right way? In other words, was the difference in Christ solely a difference in what he achieved but

191

not in anything else? The answer is that no man other than Christ could attain unto perfection. Christ was provided to do what no one else could do. The hopelessness of man is set out in a variety of places. Take, for example, the stated truth [there follows quotations from Romans 8:3 and Galatians 3:21]. Man could not keep law, and therefore righteousness could not come by law.

"We have now come to the heart of the matter. Salvation came from God. The Lord of the vineyard sent His only Son. This was the only way. Here are the critical scriptures [quotations from Romans 8:3, Galatians 4:4, John 1:14 and Luke 1:35]. No other child has ever been born in this way; Christ was God's *only* begotten. The Holy Spirit was the power which overshadowed Mary and caused her to conceive (Matthew 1:20). The Son of God did not exist before he was born of Mary; he was *born* of her. He was 'made under the law' and not outside of or above it. Nevertheless, he was truly God's Son; God was his Father. It was for this reason that he is said to have come down from heaven. There would have been no Son of God had not God moved. His word, his divine intent hitherto made known in mighty promises, was now made operative by His Spirit, and Christ was conceived, 'not ... of the will of man, but of God' (John 1:13).

"It must be made clear that Jesus was not called Son of God because of things external to his person, the circumstances around him, for example; he was Son of God in his actual being because he was begotten of the Father by the Spirit ... 'Therefore also that holy thing which shall be born of thee shall be called the Son of God' (Luke 1:35). There has never been such a child from conception to birth."[3]

The whole article referred to above is recommended. It includes a pertinent paragraph by Brother Robert

---

3 Brother Harry Tennant, "The Nature of Christ", *The Testimony*, July 1988, pages 235,236.

Roberts who advises against asking the 'how' questions, on the grounds of impracticability and folly; it is more useful to ask the 'why' questions, and never more so than in this matter of God working the miracle of the virgin birth to produce His own Son.

Exactly how Jesus did what he did, we do not know, and as far as we are concerned, it is not revealed, or important for us to know. That is a matter between the Father and the Son. The fact remains, he did achieve a supreme victory over all temptation. We thank God that he did so triumphantly.

Temptations intensified

Being God's Son made Jesus different. If the miraculous begettal provided him with some advantages in assisting him to be a sinless bearer of our condemned nature, then the severity of his trials and temptations which followed in the ministry were far in excess of what we experience, will have to face, or can possibly imagine. It was inevitable. Given that Jesus "knew what was in man", he was more aware of his surroundings, especially the challenges to his disciples and the personal dangers to himself. Whatever situations he faced, his answers always needed to be truthful and true, as he presented the Gospel in exhortation, miracle or parable to his hearers.

Unbelievably, and notwithstanding the generosity of the things he did and said, he was watched and spied on; reported to the authorities; contradicted and ridiculed; insulted and hurt by the barbs and shafts of his detractors' words. As each day passed when "his hour was not yet come", he could not relax his calling and forfeit God's glory. He was misunderstood either deliberately or through ignorance. His words were twisted against him. He was asked trick questions, with the intention of undermining his integrity, and deflecting him off course. He was held to be an imposter and called a blasphemer. But he was "the Son of man whom [God] made strong for [Himself]".

His control in remaining totally calm in the face of unwarranted provocation is the measure of his love for and faith in God, as well as his compassion for dying mankind: it was because he understood the great concept of salvation he was to accomplish; because he knew his Father was in him "reconciling the world unto himself"; because he appreciated all too keenly what an unfulfilled purpose of redemption would mean. One can only wonder at the intensity of the opposing forces and the strength of character revealed by the Son.

He left the crowds and even the twelve at intervals to go to the mountains to pray, both alone and lonely, to seek the wisdom from above; to find answers to his questions and solutions to his dilemmas. He went to find the strength, for example, to resist a misguided invitation to be their King, when he was already their King and kingship would be given at some point in time.

The gravity of the ministry temptations was heightened just because he was the Son of God, with unimaginable power in his hands. But his heart stayed true. His mind remained focused on his Father's will. He set his face "steadfastly ... to go to Jerusalem" and did not deviate off course. Had he not vowed, "I delight to do thy will, O my God: yea, thy law is within my heart" (Psalm 40:8)? He would do it – but at what cost to himself.

"[Jesus] in the days of his flesh, when he had offered up prayers and supplications with strong crying and tears unto him that was able to save him from death, and was heard in that he feared; though he were a Son, yet learned he obedience by the things which he suffered; and being made perfect, he became the author of eternal salvation unto all them that obey him."   (Hebrews 5:7,8)

Given that Jesus could only accomplish what he did because he was the Christ, the Son of the Living God, it will be useful for us to look again at the scriptures to see how these could have assisted him to be the kind of man he was, and the Saviour he needed to be, and thankfully became with God's help.

16

BLESSED IS THE MAN THAT ENDURES TEMPTATION

SCRIPTURE principles in action form our next consideration of the Lord's response to temptation. We review four important aspects of the spiritual education and development of Jesus that may have helped him in his conquering of sin and temptation, namely: Precepts, Visions, Teaching and Practice.

Precepts	The maxims, and the moral instruction in the Old Testament which would offer encouragement, help and hope to Jesus as he began his life of faith, from the earliest age.
Visions	The visions of end-time glory as described in the Old Testament which would provide his motivation. They explain why the sacrificial life was essential and expected, why it was worthwhile and would achieve great and mighty things.
Teaching	How Jesus incorporated into his teaching about discipleship the principles learned from the Old Testament precepts. It explains his focus and determination, and his awareness that much was to be accomplished to fulfil his Father's purpose of redemption.
Practice	Identifies that the strength of the Lord is seen in the way the precepts, visions and teaching are worked out in daily life, his life of love.

Precepts

These are the maxims, moral instruction and guidance for living. To illustrate, we shall look at a number of Proverbs and see how this teaching could have guided the mind and life of Jesus. The Proverbs are the instruction of a Father for His Son who is destined for great and mighty things – the kingship over Israel, God's people and the world.

"There is a way that seemeth right unto a man, but the end thereof are the ways of death."

(Proverbs 16:25)

There is a stark choice to be made. The passage sets out the alternatives. It goes back to the problem introduced into the world by the serpent, which deceived Eve and trapped Adam. This is the place where two ways meet, and it's a continuing battle, between the flesh and the spirit, the carnal mind and spiritual mind. Jesus faced this choice every day and needed to confirm his decision to fulfil all righteousness, both to himself and to his Father, as the unending temptations of the ways of men pressed in upon him. They were successfully resisted and repudiated.

Now the second proverb:

"For that they hated knowledge, and did not choose the fear of the LORD: they would none of my counsel: they despised all my reproof. Therefore shall they eat of the fruit of their own way, and be filled with their own devices. For the turning away of the simple shall slay them, and the prosperity of fools shall destroy them." (1:29-32)

These verses describe some of the experiences and challenges of the ministry. But the rebuffs had come early in the life of Jesus, when he was rejected and alienated by his "mother's children" (Psalm 69:8), and treated as an outcast and held to be "beside himself" (Mark 3:21). It was Genesis 3 re-enacted in his own life. The passage has echoes of the Eden travesty when the serpent triumphed in the words – 'eat your own fruit, go your own way, scheme your own devices; the simple,

197

slay them; fools, destroy them'. It is about the folly of making wrong choices.

We can link this with the next example:

"She is a tree of life to them that lay hold upon her: and happy is every one that retaineth her."

(Proverbs 3:18)

The reference to the tree of life directs us to Genesis 2. There is also a description of wisdom from Proverbs 3:13 onwards. We are presented with a contrast in these last two passages: namely, the folly of making wrong choices which brings destruction, and the wisdom of the right way providing access to the tree of life. The Father's instruction to the Son emphasises the benefits and therefore the urgent need of finding "wisdom that is from above". The next proverb takes us into a private family gathering:

"Hear, ye children, the instruction of a father, and attend to know understanding. For I give you good doctrine, forsake ye not my law. For I was my father's son, tender and only beloved in the sight of my mother. He taught me also, and said unto me, Let thine heart retain my words: keep my commandments, and live. Get wisdom, get understanding: forget it not; neither decline from the words of my mouth. Forsake her not, and she shall preserve thee: love her, and she shall keep thee. Wisdom is the principal thing; therefore get wisdom: and with all thy getting get understanding ... Hear, O my son, and receive my sayings; and the years of thy life shall be many. I have taught thee in the way of wisdom; I have led thee in right paths. When thou goest, thy steps shall not be straitened; and when thou runnest, thou shalt not stumble. Take fast hold of instruction: let her not go: keep her; for she is thy life."

(Proverbs 4:1-7,10-13)

These are words of encouragement written by a loving Father to his beloved Son. We can easily appreciate that these were written with the Lord Jesus Christ in mind. We have a picture of Father and Son having an earnest conversation in the Son's formative years, about the best direction to take in life and what will profit most. There is urgency in the Father's voice, a mutual love and respect the one for the other. He calls him "tender" and "beloved", for he is an only precious Son whose good and profitable life would make his Father glad. His Father taught him; His word will add years to the Son's life, and lead him in right ways. Here is the promise of support in the difficult times ahead. More than that, these words, this wisdom, is his life. It is clearly not just about the daily earthly life of a mere thirty-three years, but the basis of eternal kingdom life.

Now the fifth reference:

"My son, if thou wilt *receive* my words, and *hide* my commandments with thee; so that thou *incline* thine ear unto wisdom, and *apply* thine heart to understanding; yea, if thou *criest after* knowledge, and *liftest up* thy voice for understanding; if thou *seekest* her as silver, and *searchest* for her as for hid treasures; then shalt thou understand the fear of the LORD, and find the knowledge of God. For the LORD giveth wisdom: out of his mouth cometh knowledge and understanding." (Proverbs 2:1-6)

The Father describes eight different activities. They are italicised for emphasis. These are the mining operations to discover the treasures of the word of God. This is the stuff of application, the work of endeavour, the patience of the search. In the end, the word reveals its treasures, and they are rich and incomparable – the fear of the Lord and the knowledge of God. This was the life of Jesus. He lived in the presence of God, acknowledged his Father's constant daily care, realising he was known through and through. This understanding sustained him and provided for all his needs. The expression in verse 6, "out of his mouth", reminds us of Deuteronomy 8:3, that "man doth not live by bread only, but by every word that proceedeth out of the mouth of the LORD".

Visions

As an objective to encourage the hard sacrificial life of Jesus, God provided pictures of what was to come. These were kingdom visions to support the faithful life, when not only would the redemption of men and women be complete, but the Father Himself would be established and acknowledged as the supreme sovereign once again, and be all in all.

But first, as the Father had poured into His Son's open ears, morning by morning, words of comfort and faith, as we saw in Isaiah 50, what was the meaning of these words by the same prophet when he said, "he poured out his soul unto death"?

"Therefore will I divide him a portion with the great, and he shall divide the spoil with the strong; because he hath poured out his soul unto death: and he was numbered with the transgressors; and he bare the sin of many, and made intercession for the transgressors." (Isaiah 53:12)

Have we considered Jesus' thoughts when he read this portion of the scroll and perhaps at first didn't fully understand it, and puzzled what it meant? He would ask his Father the same question put by the Ethiopian eunuch to Philip, "Of whom speaketh the prophet this? of himself, or of some other man?" And the reply would have been the same, 'Not of himself, but some other man, my Son. Actually it's about you, this is your life; this is what you will accomplish for me'. What thoughts would race through the mind of Jesus, trying to cope with the enormity of what was written about him, and coming to terms with all the implications of the words of the prophet? He was grappling with the violence and horror of his death. Was this really what his Father wanted for him? And this is only one of the many pictures drawn by the Old Testament to prepare and encourage Jesus in the non-rebellious and obedient life, of which Isaiah 50 spoke.

Now another picture, with an entirely different scene, yet equally part of the same work. The kingdom is being established:

"Thou shalt arise, and have mercy upon Zion: for the time to favour her, yea, the set time, is come. For thy servants take pleasure in her stones, and favour the dust thereof. So the heathen shall fear the name of the LORD, and all the kings of the earth thy glory. When the LORD shall build up Zion, he shall appear in his glory."   (Psalm 102:13-16)

These are promises of victory and prospects of personal exaltation and glory. They are to be shared by "the generation to come: and the people which shall be created and shall praise the LORD" (verse 18). This is the new creation of God redeemed from death, Jesus himself being the firstborn. The joy of the fulfilment of the Father's purpose is described later in this psalm. We see a pen-picture of what is to be and glimpse some of its richness. The colours are lacklustre in the shadow, waiting for the brightness of the Son to illuminate them. But the promise is there and would be understood by Jesus as he read the psalm, which began with an account of his desolation and the pressures of his ministry. He would be encouraged.

Isaiah 53 and Psalm 102 are just two of the many pictures and visions in the Old Testament which provided motivation and comfort for Jesus in his ministry, and contributed to his determination to be victorious over temptation. They are the objectives for the selfless life. Although entirely different in their presentation of the purpose of God and kingdom glory, both were equally important in the life of Jesus to assist him to accomplish what he needed to do.

His fundamental teaching

We have been concerned with the temptations of Jesus, and particularly the way in which they were presented in the wilderness, that is (1) to turn the stones into bread, (2) the leap from the pinnacle of the temple, and (3) taking the kingdoms of the world. They feature prominently in his teaching as well as confronting him in his daily life. We saw earlier how they were repeated, quite randomly but frequently, until the very last moments of his natural life.

As we explore the teaching of Jesus we shall see how determined he was to impress upon his disciples the same lessons he had learned himself – particularly those lessons about the horror and evil of sin, and the wisdom of a serious effort to overcome personal weaknesses. The answers he gave in the wilderness to the tempter when he was oppressed are reinforced in his ministry teaching to emphasise the importance of godly thinking and living. We shall consider briefly in the light of this teaching the three temptations, and will look at Matthew 5 and the Sermon on the Mount.

"Blessed are they which do hunger and thirst after righteousness: for they shall be filled" (verse 6). This is about being fed and is an indirect reference to the first temptation. We are reminded that "man doth not live by bread only, but by every word that proceedeth out of the mouth of the LORD" (Deuteronomy 8:3). Jesus emphasises the importance of the spiritual bread of life and where energies ought to be directed.

"Blessed are the pure in heart: for they shall see God" (verse 8). This is the antithesis of the leap from the pinnacle of the temple, for this temptation concerns the pride of life, a 'me first and look at me' attitude. These are idols in the heart, and it cannot be a pure heart which harbours idols. "The heart is deceitful above all things, and desperately wicked." To be pure in heart is to evict the idol to prevent it doing the spectacular, and put in its place the honour of God.

"Blessed are the poor in spirit: for theirs is the kingdom of heaven" (verse 3), and "Blessed are the meek: for they shall inherit the earth" (verse 5). These two verses are alluding to the problem of taking "the kingdoms of the world", because this temptation promotes the lust of the eyes, and a grasping attitude. To be poor in spirit and meek and lowly in heart, is the very opposite of the selfish attitude which would claim honours and glory before the appointed time, even though they might be due. The kingdom would come to the one who had developed the contrite and humble spirit of dependence and trust in the Lord, and waited for His time. That hour would come, as Jesus himself had said.

The first temptation and its endless possibilities are taught in Matthew 7, as follows:

"What man is there of you, whom if his son ask bread, will he give him a stone? or if he ask a fish, will he give him a serpent? If ye then, being evil, know how to give good gifts unto your children, how much more shall your Father which is in heaven give good things to them that ask him?"   (verses 9-11)

This is an indirect reference to turning stones into bread, the lust of the flesh and material gain. Jesus is concerned to emphasise the importance of the power of prayer and believing that God will provide in His own time, and in our best interests. It's about having the wisdom to believe that man should live by every word which proceeds out of the mouth of the Lord, knowing and accepting there will only be good things.

What follows is a series of verses about prayer, being the vehicle Jesus used to cultivate the resources of faith which helped him to combat the temptations of his life. This faith was reinforced by a confidence in the knowledge and understanding of God, as he simply explained:

"But when ye pray, use not vain repetitions, as the heathen do: for they think that they shall be heard for their much speaking. Be not ye therefore like unto them: for your Father knoweth what things ye have need of, before ye ask him."   (6:7,8)

Given that the Father created everything, sustains everything, is everywhere present, and is all powerful beyond our imagination or understanding, it is quite credible that Jesus should say our Father knows what we have need of before we ask Him. This should comfort us whatever response from God there is, for it will be for our ultimate blessing and salvation. It might not be what we expected, or wanted, but it will be what we really need. In the wisdom of God, He will provide it. We must never say that God does not answer our prayers, because He always does. Of that we are in no doubt. What we probably mean, if we challenge God's response, is that we are disappointed with God's gift when He answered our prayer, and He didn't give us what we had prayed for.

We move forward in time to the Tuesday of the last week of the earthly life of Jesus, when he withered the fig tree:

"Jesus answered and said unto them, Verily I say unto you, If ye have faith, and doubt not, ye shall not only do this which is done to the fig tree, but also if ye shall say unto this mountain, Be thou removed, and be thou cast into the sea; it shall be done. And all these things, whatsoever ye shall ask in prayer, believing, ye shall receive." (Matthew 21:21,22)

This is certainly elevating the practice of prayer and the power of faith and most, if not all, of us have now been left far behind, wondering about withered trees and mountains moving into the sea. Sometimes we explain this and say, 'Well, Jesus didn't really mean this, it's just a figure of speech; he doesn't expect us to have this kind of faith, and why would we want to change the geography of the landscape anyway?' But this is not quite the thrust of verse 21: "if ye have faith and doubt not"; and verse 22: "all things, whatsoever ye shall ask".

Leaving this aside, but accepting that Jesus did mean what he said about prayer and promised about faith to his disciples, it tells us that Jesus was so different from the rest of us. His words underscore that we lack the type of faith referred to here, and that we should be constrained to say, "Lord, [we] believe; help thou [our] unbelief". This is also an indicator as to why Jesus was able to resist temptation, and we often cannot. His capacity for faith in the promise and willingness of his Father to come to his aid when he prayed was so much greater than ours. We remain rooted to the spot, as it were, as Jesus strides ahead. We hardly follow in this aspect of our spiritual journey.

Next, we chronologically move back about twelve months before the cross and to the events immediately after the transfiguration:

'Then came the disciples to Jesus apart, and said, Why could not we cast him out? And Jesus said unto them, Because of your unbelief: for verily I say unto you, If ye have faith as a grain of mustard seed, ye shall say unto this mountain, Remove hence to yonder place; and it shall remove; and nothing shall be impossible unto you. Howbeit this kind goeth not out but by prayer and fasting." (Matthew 17:19-21)

This comment was made due to the disciples' failure to heal the epileptic boy while Jesus, Peter, James and John were sharing the wonder of the transfiguration. There is a reference again to mountains being moved. The cause of their failure, as explained by Jesus for presumably the disciples had the power, is accounted for by (1) unbelief; (2) miracles are impossible without faith; (3) prayer and fasting are essential elements. This passage is very challenging, and it is nigh impossible to rise to it. But it sets the Lord Jesus apart as a man of towering faith.

If we consider verse 21, is this how he was successful in defeating temptation in the wilderness – that for forty days he fasted, while engaged in prayer? We know from the Gospel records he didn't eat anything during that time, and only at the end "angels came and ministered unto him". There is nothing explicit about fasting and prayer as a spiritual discipline in the Gospel accounts of the wilderness temptations, but perhaps the narratives slowly released the 'secret' of his success through his teaching. In this series of references to prayer Jesus has been teaching the importance of belief in the word and the promises of God. He has been alluding to the first temptation of turning stones into bread, and explaining

205

that men must live by every word which proceeds out of the mouth of the Lord, as he did.

We shall now contemplate how the teaching of Jesus drew attention to the second temptation – the leap from the pinnacle of the temple: the pride of life; the doing of great signs and performing the spectacular to impress others when seeking for personal glory. Speaking of the scribes and Pharisees, Jesus said:

"But all their works they do for to be seen of men: they make broad their phylacteries, and enlarge the borders of their garments, and love the uppermost rooms at feasts, and the chief seats in the synagogues, and greetings in the markets, and to be called of men, Rabbi, Rabbi." (Matthew 23:5-7)

This is a sideswipe at the pride and egotism of the Pharisees and their self-promotion expressed in ostentatious standards of dress and behaviour. Clearly Jesus did not approve of their pride of life, for this was their leap from the temple pinnacle. It is the very opposite to the lifestyle which has Jesus' approval, described as follows:

"But he that is greatest among you shall be your servant. And whosoever shall exalt himself shall be abased; and he that shall humble himself shall be exalted." (verses 11,12)

This is the behaviour he would have his disciples practise: not self-abasement for self-abasement's sake, for that too is pride – but for love's sake, for the sake of service to God and for others.

The third temptation was about taking the kingdoms of the world for present gain. It was about the lust of the eyes for power and privilege. Jesus made a specific allusion to this:

"Again, the kingdom of heaven is like unto treasure hid in a field; the which when a man has found, he hideth, and for joy thereof goeth and selleth all that he hath, and buyeth that field. Again, the kingdom of heaven is like unto a merchant man, seeking goodly pearls: who, when he had found one pearl of great

price, went and sold all that he had, and bought it."
(Matthew 13:44-46)

This is straightforward and quite the opposite to the thrust of the third temptation. Each merchant and treasure seeker sold all he had to obtain the one very special treasure he had so recently discovered. He was prepared to give up everything and his life's security to gain it. It is parallel to the teaching given to the rich young ruler who was invited to sell all he had, give away to the poor, so he could follow Jesus unhindered. These illustrations are about self-sacrifice in the present, to gain the promised riches of the future. Jesus eschewed the kingdoms of the world in his day, because he was the heir of all things. Jesus is the man buying the field; he is the merchant parting with everything to gain the one pearl of great price – in his case the whole world and its kingship.

Each of these last three passages from Matthew 7, 23 and 13, has developed the teaching about temptation and its overcoming, but has dealt with the issue in a simple and direct manner. This teaching is easy to explain and understand, but hard to do.

How many of us really refuse the accolades of our peers, and therefore fail to demonstrate the humility looked for by the Lord Jesus, because in our hearts and minds, as well as in practice, we leap from the temple pinnacle to impress others? How many of us have really sacrificed everything we hold precious for the Gospel's sake, and have not secretly retained some of the old ways of the flesh, and therefore in our hearts have tarnished the pearl of great price and diminished its value? Our attitude and answers must be honest. When we look back to what was and wish for more of yesterday's bread it is not helpful, as the Children of Israel discovered when they left Egypt and complained about their diet.

"As they went in the way, a certain man said unto him, Lord, I will follow thee whithersoever thou goest. And Jesus said unto him, Foxes have holes, and birds of the air have nests; but the Son of man hath not where to lay his head. And he said unto another, Follow me, But he said, Lord, suffer me first to go and bury my father. Jesus said unto him, Let the dead bury their dead: but go thou and preach the kingdom of God. And another also said, Lord, I will follow thee; but let me first go bid them farewell, which are at home at my house. And Jesus said unto him, No man, having put his hand to the plough, and looking back, is fit for the kingdom of God."

(Luke 9:57-62)

We recognise the good example of Elisha and the poor one of Lot's wife in this passage. Furthermore, the responses of the three people in the story are instructive. Each said, "I will follow thee" but made their own conditions. "Let me first ..." – as if they were doing Jesus a favour by becoming his disciples! Jesus had no roof over his head, and none of this world's goods, but he possessed the pearl of great price. The would-be followers, by holding on to what they trusted in, declared them to be more important and valuable than the prize offered through the work of Jesus. The value of the prize was unknown to them; but they lacked the faith to think outside their secure and familiar comfort zones. Launching out into the deep was not for them. They needed a paradigm shift.

Jesus was not making a point about the natural world or ploughing fields, but about seeking first the kingdom of God, whatever the cost. He had no bed; he had left his family to be about his Father's business; he had not returned home since the day of his baptism. Now he taught the urgency and value of discipleship, and by personal experience knew the privations and the cost involved. Could his potential followers match this? Clearly some couldn't.

We have seen in this short exploration some of Jesus' teaching and how it focused on the positive aspects of living, to provide antidotes to the waywardness of the flesh and the danger of falling into temptation. It addressed the problem of temptation in quite a subtle and gentle way. It is one thing to teach, but quite another to do it.

Practice

Jesus' living example shows us that he had an awareness of the problems of daily living, and that these significantly increased as the cross came closer. This is what we shall look at now.

"He steadfastly set his face"

"The Son of man must suffer many things, and be rejected of the elders and chief priests and scribes, and be slain, and be raised the third day."

(Luke 9:22)

Jesus only revealed his suffering to the twelve when they understood and confessed he was "the Christ, the Son of the living God", as Peter did in verse 20 (see also Matthew 16:16). This was followed by instruction concerning the taking up of the cross daily, denying self and confessing him as Lord and Saviour. That point would be very grave, given their knowledge and eyewitness experience of Roman crucifixion. Luke then describes the transfiguration with all its wonder about glory and kingship, to confirm that Jesus was at the heart of the redemptive purpose, as the voice out of the cloud restated. At verse 51 the journey south to Jerusalem began. It was about twelve months to the cross.

"When the time was come that he should be received up, he steadfastly set his face to go to Jerusalem." (verse 51)

Luke is describing the resolve of Jesus "when the time was come"; so he began a journey which would end in the ascension, "that he should be received up". So he is still kingdom focused. The Greek for "received up" (*analepsis*) comes from a root meaning 'to take up', and could be applied to the ascension being the ultimate hopeful purpose. Luke then gives a sequence of nine references to show the determination of Jesus in getting

209

to Jerusalem to accomplish this great undertaking (these are: 9:53; 13:22; 17:11; 18:31; 19:1,11,28,41,45 – he had arrived).

The phrase "steadfastly set his face" comes from Isaiah 50:7, which we looked at earlier. There the prophet wrote: "I have set my face like a flint, and I know that I shall not be ashamed". This was the final journey. There is no doubt that Jesus fought a dreadful painful battle with himself as he approached Jerusalem. He agonised and was exceedingly sorrowful. It was not an easy battle to win. Yet he had gained the victory three times already in the wilderness of temptation, and how many more times during the ministry?

17

I HAVE OVERCOME THE WORLD

"I have a baptism to be baptized with; and how am I straitened till it be accomplished!"   (Luke 12:50)

THE word "straitened" is opened up in the AV margin as "pained". But Jesus' situation was far beyond daily anxiety or normal worry. This was real stress, a tribulation which was pressing heavily upon him and of very serious concern. It was stress beyond measure and really hurting to bear it. This was a 'no way out' situation. His prospect was death. This is what his baptism in the River Jordan had meant. 'Allow it, for it is fitting for us to fulfil all righteousness'. That vow made before God now needed to be fulfilled, but it drew out of Jesus all his resolve, all his heart, soul, mind, and strength. He emptied himself as he "poured out his soul unto death".

There is a succession of six references in Luke, including this one, using the same Greek word *sunecho*. They all describe 'stress beyond measure' circumstances, where the end result, more often than not, was death. It is a very powerful word and is used only in extreme situations. It means, inter alia, 'being consumed by, pressured, pressed in on; surrounded by, constrained, compelled, overwhelmed, to be taken with'. There is a passion, it's painful, and therefore 'pained'; a concentration of force, fear and pain. That is why Jesus was "pained", mentally, physically and emotionally.

There are another six references of this same Greek word *sunecho* outside the Gospel of Luke, and for the sake of completeness these twelve passages are tabulated, as follows:

211

Reference	English AV
Luke 4:38	taken with
Luke 8:37	were taken with
Luke 8:45	throng
Luke 12:50	am straitened
Luke 19:43	keep in
Luke 22:63	that held
Matthew 4:24	that were taken with
Acts 7:57	stopped
Acts 18:5	was pressed
Acts 28:8	[Publius] sick of
2 Corinthians 5:14	constraineth
Philippians 1:23	am in a strait

So for Jesus, the accomplishment of this baptism meant that he was consumed by its total importance and relevance to the needs of his people. He felt great pressure to be victorious, both over all his temptations and in the completion of the divine purpose. He felt constrained to fulfil the work. He was held by that purpose and greatly taken with it. Each day there was a dividing of the ways, a crossroads to face, decisions to be made. But these decisions were so personal and self-sacrificing, so painful and passionate, and so all-consuming as he saw the prospects of his passion ahead, that it presented him with his greatest and most difficult choice. That choice would come even before the cross, before the time when he would feel the nails. But there was no relaxation of his grip on this baptism, nor would he diminish the heavenly declaration made at his water baptism, "In thee I am well pleased". His strength of mind was evident when he proceeded with the final stage of his calling.

212

Jesus taught his followers to be single-minded; to have specific goals centred on God's ways, and to be focused on the kingdom. This is what he practised day by day. He steadfastly set his face and had a baptism to be baptized with. It pained him.

"Moved with compassion"

There is another dimension to the accomplishment of his Father's objectives. Jesus' earnestness in fulfilling the baptism by which he was straitened, and being obedient to the heavenly voice, was not only driven by his having to overcome mental and emotional stress. It drew from him yearning and pity; not for himself as might be the case with this baptism, but for men and women suffering the bondage of sin.

The Gospels tell us more than once that Jesus was "moved with compassion" for the multitudes. Whereas "moved with compassion" is basically a physical word, it is also an emotional one concerned with deep inner feelings towards those held captive by the human condition. "Moved with compassion" is the translation of the Greek verb *splagchnizomai*, which means 'to feel sympathy for and to pity; to have inward affections and tender mercies towards those who are needy and desperate'. The noun (always plural) is *splagchnon*, meaning 'the bowels, the heart, the liver, literally the inward parts'. The word is used, for example, in Luke 1:78, Philippians 2:1, Colossians 3:12 and Philemon verses 7,12,20. The bowels were regarded as the seat of the tender affections, especially kindness, benevolence, compassion – hence our heart.

When the Gospels tell us Jesus was "moved with compassion" towards the people, we are being informed that he had great sympathy and inner feelings for them, which came from deep within him. He yearned and perhaps agonized because of what he knew, and saw and felt for the people. He was the one specially chosen by God to resolve these problems. It would be at a personal cost, but the freedom and release from death for countless numbers was the prize. We explored in

213

Chapter 1 how utterly devastating is the mortality we bear and the insidious nature of temptation. The Lord knew its force, because he, like the rest of us, was caught up in its serpentine tentacles leading to death, unless there was a remedy.

> "But when [Jesus] saw the multitudes, he was moved with compassion on them, because they fainted, and were scattered abroad, as sheep having no shepherd."　　　　　　　　　　(Matthew 9:36)

In Matthew chapters 8 and 9, the Gospel writer brings together a collection of healing miracles to demonstrate how Jesus met the people's needs, and refers to Isaiah 53:4: "himself took our infirmities, and bare our sicknesses" (Matthew 8:17). What closer identification could there be? Jesus had been working in the Galilee district and this work was summed up as "Jesus ... healing every sickness and every disease among the people" (9:35). This involvement was motivated by his compassion. The multitudes were weary and harassed. They were leaderless, "as sheep having no shepherd" or as one writer puts it, "feeling as if they had no shepherd". They were bereft of spiritual and moral guidance, bearing burdens which were unbearable, having formless but formal religious duties to perform. These were sterile and provided no comfort in the renewal and expression of faith. In addition to this, the people were subject to the iron oppression of Rome. Jesus recognised that even this desperate situation could yield a ready and responsive harvest when he declared it to be plenteous. The people were ripe for the Gospel message, but an important element of this was the practical demonstration of its spiritual principles. The Apostle James was to write in a similar vein in James 2:14-17. It is the same today.

Matthew next describes the calling of the twelve, the gift of power they were given, and the commission to preach the kingdom, and to heal all sicknesses and all manner of diseases following the pattern set by Jesus. His love for his neighbours was truly manifested, in spite of blind unwarranted criticism and opposition from the self-appointed religious shepherds of the nation.

Jesus dealt with people on the basis of their individual faith and need. In a sense it was left to the individual to state his need and express his belief in the person and work of Jesus. This is powerfully illustrated by the meeting between two blind men and the Lord Jesus outside Jericho. The fact that Jesus was followed through and out of the city by "a great multitude" of people adds poignancy to this remarkable scene, that Jesus should hear, see and call two blind men to him. Of all the number on the road, some would undoubtedly have had needs of one kind or another, but it is only recorded of these two apparently inconsequential beggars that they had a faith which they were not afraid to declare publicly despite rebuke. They also boldly confessed their need. Matthew tells us:

"Jesus had compassion on them, and touched their eyes: and immediately their eyes received sight, and they followed him." (Matthew 20:34)

The witness made by the two blind beggars, one of whom was Bartimaeus (Mark 10:46), drew from Jesus his deep-seated feelings of compassion and love. The blind men felt the gentle touch of kindness on their unseeing eyes and immediately received their sight. It does not mean that Jesus had no compassion for the great number of people who followed him, or that Bartimaeus and his sightless companion were worthier or holier than all the rest. Of course not! The incident teaches that faith in the person of Jesus and his part in the fulfilment (in this case) of the Davidic covenant, coupled with an honest recognition of personal weaknesses and need, is a benchmark of confession.

One of the more heart-rending episodes in the ministry of Jesus came early on in the healing of a nameless leper. All three synoptic Gospels describe both the sadness and the joy when Jesus touched the leprous man to heal him (Matthew 8:2-4; Mark 1:40-45;

Luke 5:12-16). Only Mark uses the word *splagchnizomai* – "moved with compassion" to describe Jesus' feelings:

> "And there came a leper to him, beseeching him, and kneeling down to him, and saying unto him, If thou wilt, thou canst make me clean. And Jesus, moved with compassion, put forth his hand, and touched him, and saith unto him, I will; be thou clean. And as soon as he had spoken, immediately the leprosy departed from him, and he was cleansed." (Mark 1:40-42)

Again, Jesus was in Galilee and moving between towns. It appears he was met whilst on the road by a desperately sick man "full of leprosy", who had come out of isolation. There is no inference that he was supported by friends or accompanied by others, who might have testified for him. He was alone and undoubtedly lonely. But he had heard of Jesus.

The conversation between the leper and the Lord of Life begins with what sounds like a challenge: "If thou wilt ..." It was not a challenge. It was an unreserved and unambiguous confession of faith in the ability and power of Jesus to heal. The leper was kneeling and worshipping. All the ingredients of what was needed were present. The confession was sincere and his plight plain to see.

Jesus could have responded with a great commanding word to effect the much needed cure. That would have been dramatic enough, but the Lord of Love extended himself by reaching out and touching the diseased man. What the accompanying crowd thought is not recorded; they had a fixed mindset about the treatment of lepers who were expelled from society, having no contact with others. But Jesus' touch had an immediate effect and the man was made clean. We can only imagine what yearning and emotion this poor man drew out of the Lord.

Jesus' close involvement and identification with afflicted people when he "took our infirmities and bare our sicknesses" is referred to by Mark when he recorded, after the incident and because of unwanted publicity, that Jesus "was without in desert places" (Mark 1:45). This was the very place from which the leper had come and in which other lepers lived! Ironically those who shunned the leper and his dwelling place "came to [Jesus] from every quarter": now unafraid and expectant, or curious, or fault finding.

Only Luke tells of the raising from the dead of the widow of Nain's son. She was now left alone. On the face of it she was unsupported and vulnerable. The breadwinner was dead. But it was a divine injunction to look after the fatherless and the widow, and many times in the Old Testament there is firm emphasis on supporting this unprotected and vulnerable class of people, with a corresponding condemnation if they were ignored. It was a first principle.

Jesus' arrival at Nain just as the funeral party were progressing to the burial spot, was not a coincidence. Jesus knew that such an event would take place and his arrival was precisely at the right time. Jesus was always in control. He was accompanied by his disciples and "much people", who would be the witnesses of the miracle about to happen:

> "And when the Lord saw her, he had compassion on her, and said unto her, Weep not. And he came and touched the bier: and they that bare him stood still. And he said, Young man, I say unto thee, Arise." (Luke 7:13,14)

The circumstances of widowhood had been compounded by the death of an only child. Luke describes the situation carefully with the accuracy of the historian and medical practitioner. He missed nothing: the emotion of the occasion, the undoubted pathos of the mourners, the tear stained red-eyed face of the mother. Jesus would see all this. But he does not judge by the sight of his eyes or the hearing of his ears. He sees straight into the heart. What he saw moved him with compassion and he touched the open coffin. Like the earlier time when he touched the leper, he was now physically connected

217

with the coffin of the dead. According to the law this act made him ritually and physically unclean. The recorded words that passed between the principal characters were brief, but enough: "Weep not"; "Young man, I say unto thee, Arise."

The crisis was over, but the drama was just beginning. The dead man sat up, spoke and was delivered to his mother. The rejoicing would be indescribable. Luke's narrative does not tell what was said by the widowed mother. She was walking ahead of the bier, being comforted by the mourning women and the pain of death would lie heavily on her heart. What Jesus did happened behind her, after the bearers had stopped for a moment. This would not be unusual as different bearers would take turns to carry the dead man. Only a moment was required. The needs of one vulnerable widow, the witness made by the travelling crowds, the impact on the inhabitants of Nain, Galilee and Judaea – all were satisfied in this fleeting moment, as the young man came back from the dead. The silent cries of yearning hearts in desperate prayers met at Nain. The motivation was compassion and a love moved by deep seated-emotion. It was true sympathy. The people glorified God.

These incidents demonstrate the care which Jesus took over individuals and their circumstances. They are a fulfilment of that remarkable prophecy in Luke 4 when the Lord had completed his reading from Isaiah 61, "This day is this scripture fulfilled in your ears". Over the next three-and-a-half years the scripture was fulfilled before their eyes, in that the poor, the broken-hearted, the captives, the blind and the bruised, had the Gospel of peace preached to them. They were healed, delivered and set at liberty. This was Jesus conquering the forces of evil, sin and death. Cleansing people of their diseases and healing their iniquities meant the overcoming of all that was in the world, breaking the chains of afflicted souls and nullifying the serpentine behaviour of implacable enemies. Being moved with compassion was one of the major drivers which governed the Lord's relationship with his people.

Supper with his disciples

When he was only twelve hours from certain death, but before his agony in the Garden of Gethsemane, he prepared for the 'last supper', so he could be remembered. He was providing for the disciples' comfort and exhortation, as well as helping us to reappraise our lives and focus, as bread and wine are shared between us.

> "And he said unto them, With desire I have desired to eat this passover with you before I suffer: for I say unto you, I will not any more eat thereof, until it be fulfilled in the kingdom of God. And he took the cup, and gave thanks, and said, Take this, and divide it among yourselves." (Luke 22:15-17)

Some of the expressions Jesus spoke were very emphatic. "With desire": 'I have set my heart upon'; 'I have longed for this moment'. We note the double emphasis, "With desire I have desired"; that was the passion of the desire. 'With longing I have longed to'. This was a real moment to savour and share; the moment was good. Yet it was to anticipate why he was "pained". This is what he spoke about when he said, "I have a baptism to be baptized with". Now was the time of this baptism. The urgency of the moment and the solemnity of the upper room serve to emphasise the single-mindedness of Jesus in completing his baptismal vow – "to fulfil all righteousness".

He gave thanks, not only for the actual wine in the cup, but also for what it represented – his death, his atoning sacrifice, the cross, all the pain, the 'straitening' he had suffered and would yet suffer. He was perhaps giving thanks for what the Jews and Romans were about to mete out to him, and for the trials and tribulations of the previous three-and-a-half years, because it would all come together in his obedient triumphant sacrificial death, by which he would declare the righteousness of God. The sum total of all this was

219

his sacrifice and the accomplishment of all his Father had sent him to do.

It was surely a thanksgiving for being allowed to take such a crucial part in the redemption of the world, and a thanksgiving for all those who would believe on him through the word of his grace and his work. The cup had been drunk to the last drop and nothing had been allowed to fall to the ground and be left undone. All his work had been well done. The Father was well pleased. But in coming to this, the Son had been and would yet be "straitened", until all was finally accomplished.

His victory over the temptation to save himself and escape with his own life still had to be faced and won in the Garden of Gethsemane. But for the moment, in the upper room, he would share precious time with his disciples to think of salvation and the glory of the kingdom of God.

Epilogue

This brings us to the end of our exploration of the temptations of Jesus and hopefully we have reverently examined his overcoming. We have lifted the curtain a little and considered his relationship with his Father and his singular attitude of mind. We have concluded that we have not really discovered the 'secret' of his success, but gratefully acknowledge that he achieved a complete domination over the sin power.

We looked at the Old Testament scriptures which encouraged Jesus in his victory. We have explored briefly the faithfulness of his teaching, and the unwavering adherence to the high and lofty principles out of the mouth of his Father.

All this leads us to our personal appreciation of the Lord Jesus Christ, what he has done for us and how we respond to this wonderful man. He was marvellously triumphant in the mastery of self and accepted the work prepared for him by his Father from the foundation of the world. What impact does this make on us?

As we now think about Jesus, his way of life, his consideration of others both known and unknown, seen and unseen, his singular devotion to the will and pleasure of his Father at the expense of his own comfort, we remember that he had "no leisure so much as to eat". We pause in our lives and reflect on our lifestyles, and how sometimes we squander our time on transient things which we know will pass away. We excuse ourselves by saying it is the weakness of the flesh and that we need to relax from time to time, due to the busyness of our lives and crowded schedules. Whilst this is true to a degree, could we not squeeze out a little more of our time and energy for the things of God, especially in the light of what Jesus accomplished for us?

It is perhaps unhelpful to compare ourselves in minute detail with the Son of God who was a unique Son, although scripture presents him as the example to follow. We know only too well it is impossible for us to be like him, whilst in the flesh. It is the Apostle Paul who encourages his brethren and sisters when he writes, "Be ye followers of me, even as I also am of Christ" (1 Corinthians 11:1). But even Paul's exploits were considerable and well beyond the capacity of most, if not all of us.

This can leave us feeling somewhat incompetent and hopeless, if we dwell on our inability to copy precisely the doings of either Paul or Jesus; but that is not the point. In our lives of faith and faithfulness, we promised in baptism to do our best, to give of our best, and to use the gifts and graces we have been given to the best of our ability to the glory of God and the furtherance of the Gospel of Christ. We can do no more. Our circumstances, culture and environment are entirely different from our first century giants of faith, so our service will inevitably take a different course and accomplish different things. But the basics of a godly character expressed day by day will be the same. We practise the same principles laid down by both Jesus and Paul in our personal lives as well as in our ecclesias.

The inspiration for our service is the victory of Jesus in overcoming all his temptations and therefore sin, and finally death in the moment of resurrection. What he did in the constant battles against the wiles of the devil is magnificent. As convinced believers in his glorious achievements, we are left wondering that such a gracious thing could ever be contemplated, let alone completed. But it was by one who shared the weaknesses and handicaps of our poor human nature. He "abolished death and brought life and immortality to light through the gospel" (2 Timothy 1:10), and we are the beneficiaries of these things, thankfully so.

Meanwhile, as we live our God-given daily lives and recognise our inevitable failures, we have in Jesus a faithful and merciful High Priest. How good to have the Lord Jesus in this capacity, as one who understands! This is the joy of knowing that our prayers and petitions are faithfully received and acted on; and in the matter of our confessions, understood and forgiven. We are greatly encouraged and deeply moved by love to know that our sins are cast away as far as the east is from the west. We can start again with a conscience at ease with itself – at least for a little moment. We begin to know "the peace of God which passeth all understanding, [that] shall keep our hearts and minds through Christ Jesus" (Philippians 4:7). For we are reconciled to God in Christ.

Not only so, but our prospects are even more exciting. The future hope, so tantalisingly close, is anticipated as "the times of refreshing … from the presence of the Lord", and we wonder precisely what this will mean for us. This we do know, that when he comes, "we shall be like him", and we shall "be partakers of the divine nature, having escaped the corruption that is in the world through lust" (1 John 3:2; 2 Peter 1:4). What a time this will be, because of the devotions and victories over temptation and sin by the Lord Jesus Christ.

We have thought about what might have happened in the overcoming of temptation, but cannot be sure.

What we do know is that Jesus was totally triumphant – a man without equal and personal sin despite the provocations in his life. He did what no one else could. How he did it, or what his secret was, we have not discovered. There is no clear or specific answer. We are overwhelmed and deeply thankful that he achieved what he did and could say, "It is finished". But he surely leaves us breathless with wonder, and on our knees in thanksgiving and worship.

"Thanks be to God, which giveth us the victory through our Lord Jesus Christ."

(1 Corinthians 15:57)

SCRIPTURE INDEX

THE TEMPTATIONS OF JESUS

228

229